DAVID'S TRUTH

Walter
Brueggemann

DAVID'S TRUTH

IN ISRAEL'S IMAGINATION & MEMORY

Library of Congress Cataloging-in-Publication Data

Brueggemann, Walter.
   David's truth in Israel's imagination and memory.

   1. David, King of Israel—Addresses, essays, lectures.
2. Bible. O.T. Samuel—Criticism, interpretation,
etc.—Addresses, essays, lectures. I. Title.
BS580.D3B78   1985   222'.40924   85–47717
ISBN 0–8006–1865–3

1716D85   Printed in the United States of America   1–1865

For My Brother
Ed

CONTENTS

PREFACE

ALONG WITH well-established historical-critical methods, two new approaches to Old Testament study are gaining increased attention. The first of these is sociological analysis, often associated with the names of George Mendenhall, Norman K. Gottwald, Robert R. Wilson, and Paul D. Hanson. This approach attempts to understand Old Testament literature in terms of social function, the social forces that generate the literature, and the social forces in turn evoked from the literature.

The second emerging approach is literary criticism which seeks to see the text itself as offering an alternative imaginative world. Among the names associated with this perspective are Phyllis Trible, David M. Gunn, and David J. A. Clines. This approach seeks to take the text on its own terms, without reference to the social context or social world around it.

Both of these approaches hold enormous promise for future work in Scripture study. They move in opposite directions. Social analysis seeks to set the text closely *in its context*. Literary criticism seeks to let the text have its free, unfettered say, *without reference to context*. Unfortunately, each of these emerging methods has largely been utilized without much attention to the other. On the one hand, the sociologists tend not to be overly sensitive to the aesthetic realities of the text, the subtleties offered there, and the power of the text to redescribe reality in new ways. Conversely, the literary critics do not attend often enough to the social formation of the text, so that the treatment of the text sometimes becomes an interesting parlor game without realism about the world in which it is intended to function.

There is a need for these two methods to interact more seriously. As early as 1977, I urged such an interface:

> Only in the freedom of faithful speaking can the process of social criticism by bold image continue. Without the freedom of such faithful speaking, contained religion and oppressive social vision are inevitable. Thus scholarship concerned with radical social criticism informed by covenant (Mendenhall; Gottwald) needs to be more attentive to the freedom of images and the awareness that the various images in their great variety do indeed turn the central paradigm in various directions. Conversely, scholarship concerned with the meaning of language and metaphor ([Amos] Wilder; [Sallie McFague] TeSelle) needs to be more attentive to the faith which transforms every metaphor and every language in the service of the central paradigm. ("Israel's Social Criticism and Yahweh's Sexuality," Journal of the American Academy of Religion, Supplement 45/3 [1977]:765)

But not much has happened in terms of such interaction.

This book is an attempt to make use of both methods, without being enslaved to or committed to purity with either method. Obviously I have made important use of sociological analysis, generally informed by the approach of Gottwald, but particularly helped by two articles by James W. Flanagan, "Models for the Origin of Iron Age Monarchy: A Modern Case Study," Seminar Papers (Chico., Calif: Scholars Press, 1982), 135–56, and "Social Transformation and Ritual in 2 Samuel 6," in The Word of the Lord Shall Go Forth, ed. Carol L. Meyers and M. O'Connor (Winona Lake, Ind.: Eisenbrauns, 1983), 361–72. I have also made use of literary analysis, being especially influenced by David Gunn, The Story of King David, Journal for the Study of the Old Testament, Supplement 6 (Sheffield: JSOT Press, 1978), and The Fate of King Saul, Journal for the Study of the Old Testament, Supplement 14 (Sheffield: JSOT Press, 1980), but also aided by Robert Alter and J. P. Fokkelman.

But my interest is in neither social nor literary analysis and I do not intend to offer a fresh contribution to either of these approaches in any comprehensive way. Rather I have wanted to use these methods to pursue what for me is a more important and more interesting question—matters of epistemology and interpretive theory. Here I am attempting to take the Bible seriously on its own terms and to insist that every part of the text must be taken with theological seriousness. Thus I propose that "the truth of David" in the Chronicler is as important as that offered in 1 and 2 Samuel, a view not based on either the historical or literary quality of the material. Moreover, that theological seriousness is reflected in my conviction that each literary account bears truth to which we must attend.

At the same time, however, I have tried to show that the truth of the biblical text is not flat and we must not engage in reductionism or trivialization. Thus I have tried to articulate "truth" in a way resonant with the claim of the text itself which will provide no help or permit either theological reductionism with too much certitude or theological trivialization with indifference. The truth of the text is not so easily received or managed as that. My presentation is a proposal that we must wait for the text, that it may yield its claims only at its own pace, only on its own terms, and only in its own idiom. Our pace, our terms, and our idiom do not much massage the text in ways we would wish.

The making of such a book is, of course, a torturous affair, so my debts are great and my gratitude profound in many directions. In various forms the chapters have been used as lectures, at Austin Presbyterian Seminary as the Thomas White Currie Lectures, at Bangor Theological Seminary as the Francis B. Denio Lectures, and at Blacksburg Presbyterian Church as the Ellison A. Smyth Lectures. I have been graciously and caringly hosted in each place, respectively, by President Jack Maxwell, President Wayne G. Glick, and Dr. George Telford. In each case I was received in ways warm and stimulating, the last two in the midst of blizzards.

My special thanks goes to Donna LaGrasse who typed the manuscript during the throes of a pregnancy, and to Marian Reitz, my secretary, longsuffering and good humored through it all. The manuscript is measurably better, both in substance and in style, for the patient critique of my colleague, Gail R. O'Day. I am especially grateful to John A. Hollar of Fortress Press who is in every way an author's delight. He has combined enthusiasm and discipline for the manuscript which has made an important difference.

The dedication of the book is to my brother, Edward D. Brueggemann. It is in celebration of his restless faith, his dangerous candor, and his caring energy. The book is for him and all those who dare imagine truth as that which also summons us to newness. Our society currently is preoccupied with flattening and securing old truths, of putting the epistemological wagons in a circle. David stands as a summons to resist all of that for the ways of oddness where truth meets us new. My brother is in that company.

WALTER BRUEGGEMANN

Eden Theological Seminary

INTRODUCTION:
TRUTH IN ITS STRANGENESS

David IS THE dominant figure in Israel's narrative. Only Moses receives as much attention, but the narratives concerning Moses move in a very different direction. More than with any other person, Israel is fascinated by David, deeply attracted to him, bewildered by him, occasionally embarrassed by him, but never disowning him. David is one of those extraordinary historical figures who has a literary future. That is, his memory and presence keep generating more and more stories. One must, of course, recognize that others formulated those stories, perhaps even fabricated them. But surely there can be no doubt that it is David's magnificent and mysterious person that generated them, perhaps because Israel could never get it quite right. None of the stories could quite comprehend him, let alone contain him. He is a person who fits David Tracy's notion of a "classic,"[1] surrounded by a community that continually returns to him for authority, not doubting that there is more yet to be given.

PRELIMINARY CONCERNS

First of all it should be understood that we are not here interested in the "historical David," as though we could isolate and identify the real thing. That is not available to us. And even if it were, it would not be nearly so interesting or compelling as the "constructed" David that the tradition has given us.[2] What is important is that David is *the engine for Israel's imagination and for Israel's public history*. This David is no doubt a literary, imaginative construction, made by many hands. So we must settle for that. We cannot get behind the literary construction, even as we cannot get behind the construction of any significant person, and even as we cannot get behind the construction of ourselves. Because we are, all of us, imaginative constructions.[3]

In the case of David, that construction is partly deliberate, as a means of political propaganda. That cannot be doubted, though sometimes that element is more obvious than at other times. But partly that construction is inevitable and unplanned, and takes on a force and authority of its own. The portraits we have are in part generated by this magnetic memory (without intentionality) that continued to dominate the imagination of Israel. That memory simply insisted, again and again, on being given imaginative and literary form. The power of David endures, and therefore the David that emerges in these narratives is not a helpless, passive product of the artist. Rather, David is like a character in a good drama that takes on a life of his or her own and even surprises the playwright.[4] So what I seek to do, in each of these discussions, is to explore the ways in which we can participate in that David-dominated imagination, partly to participate in its ongoing work, and partly to be addressed by it.

Second, "David's truth" is my general theme. I intend that phrase to be relentlessly ambiguous, so that we do not finally know if it is the truth sponsored *about David*, in the sense of either celebration or exposé, or if it is a truth sponsored *by David*, so that it is David who makes a statement here. Indeed, in my own comments, I will probably not be consistent myself, because the force of the statement precludes such a disciplined respect for categories.

I intend to focus on the question of truth. That means I do not inquire about facticity, not what happened, but what is claimed, what is asserted here about reality. As we shall see, sometimes that assertion is obvious on the face of it, sometimes it is polemical and argumentative, insisting on this reading of reality against another. This literature, like good literature generally, is always discerning, struggling with and bringing to speech something about the truth, something about how it is with us, something that is not known in precisely this way until it is brought precisely to this articulation. So storytelling always drives us to the question of Pontius Pilate the governor, "What is truth?" (John 18:38).[5] The governor (and we along with him) asks what is reliable, what is the sure disclosure that we can count on? Our narrative does not know ahead of time what the truth of David is. Rather, the telling and hearing, the formulating and preserving and valuing and being entertained—all of that is a communal process in which the disclosure is under way.[6] Each time the tale is told, that continuing disclosure of truth is under way.

We do not ask in general about the truth, but in particular about the truth as it is linked to David's person. David is a "classic" in the sense that this community of storytelling has judged that in his person a serious, reliable disclosure of truth is offered. (Note well, it did not make the same judgment about Solomon, who is never valued as a generative source of truth.) The linkage of David and truth is not obvious or unambiguous. Sometimes David is allied with the truth, and sometimes the truth moves against David. So the truth here comes with power and with scars. But in historical narrative the truth always arrives with such ambiguous specificity. It is only people who regard the concreteness of the truth at a distance who imagine we can ever have the power of truth without the scars of truth along with it. Whatever else we are agreed upon with reference to David, even reconstructed, the community agreed that here the real truth is coming to concrete articulation, as it would not come to expression without the presence and force of this person.

Third, and finally, one ought not be surprised that the truth offered here, the man disclosed here, is not a simple unambiguous piece. Currently we say the truth is polyvalent. That is, it moves in a variety of directions and cannot be reduced to a single formulation. That rich, varied discernment is obvious as we consider the various pieces of literature that come from different hands in different contexts for different purposes. Each of them touches a dimension of this "larger-than-life" person who is surely not larger than truth. But this same polyvalent tendency is also evident in each particular narrative, because the person of David is inscrutable. And therefore the narrative must always be a bit unsure. But that is what makes a good story.

So we may ask about each text, which David? Or whose David? Two extremes may be noted. On the one hand, John McKenzie[7] characterized David as a "bloodthirsty oversexed bandit." About the same

David, Samuel Terrien[8] can say, "The purity of David's faith assumed a quality of elegance which has often gone unnoticed in modern times." We may wonder if McKenzie and Terrien are reading the same story about the same man. Perhaps the titles of the books are useful: McKenzie is concerned with the Old Testament "without illusion," Terrien writes of the "elusive presence." It is provocative to play with their two words: *illusion* and *elusive*. McKenzie poses a flat, historical question in an attempt to break open the romantic pretense involved in so much popular Scripture study. Terrien in a much more subtle way allows for the shadow of the inscrutable. Obviously, how the question is posed will make a difference in the telling. And neither McKenzie nor Terrien fully answers the wistful question of the Roman governor, "What is truth?" Because finally the Bible makes the truth available only as narrative,[9] even if we want more. The truth comes relentlessly packaged in ambiguity, inscrutability, polyvalence. The revealed truth is always continually hidden and we are left to be amazed and chagrined. If one follows the scholarship of McKenzie and Terrien, one may understand why each has put the question as he has, and how the putting of the question of the truth yields a certain kind of answer. So our purpose in exposition is never to eliminate the hiddenness, for that is to want to know too much. Such analysis that leaves nothing to the imagination is indeed pornographic.[10] Rather, our stance is to wait in that very hiddenness for seasons of disclosure. We may look for pure faith and be surprised to find a bandit. We may look for "the truth" and find only David. Or we may seek for David and be surprised at meeting the truth. One never knows. The storyteller intends us never to know for sure. Indeed likely the storyteller does not always know either.

The Truths About David

This discussion is preoccupied with David. It has no other purpose in view. But it is worth noting at the outset that I treat David as something of a paradigm, as I think ancient Israel understood.[11] That is, in what we are able to say of David's truth, here we may know truth more generally and indeed we may know the truth concerning ourselves. Thus each of these three preliminary points permits generalization.

In the first place, historical persons are never "historical" but always constructions and portraits, partly done for us and to us, and partly done by ourselves, as we are always busily constructing ourselves for the sake of appearance and for the sake of self-understanding. Those constructions are characteristically strange combinations of fidelity and deception.

In the second place, the question of truth in life does not yield to scientific certitude. Our exegetical methods have sometimes done us a disservice in this regard. In our modern world, we so easily imagine that truth has to do with facticity, and then the religious community is busied with certitude. But the truth of David here yields no certitude, certainly not any facticity, but nonetheless glimpses of reality. That is how it always is, though we struggle with technical reason. These narrators understood, and so can we, that our truth always comes with scars.

Last, the truth about ourselves and all of life is finally polyvalent. How odd it is that the biblical text knows this best! Yet in the name of this very biblical text there are those who deny the polyvalent character of truth. But we do know, in our moments of discernment, that where such a polyvalent quality in truth is crushed, we likely have ideology that is in the service of someone's special agenda. Thus, about ourselves as about David and about Jesus, the Roman administrator could not have the kind of answer he wanted to his question, for he wanted the kind of truth that would pass muster in the Roman government. There are, of course, many today who want the same kind of truth and for much the same reason. But such truth is not available to us in these texts, nor, I suspect, anywhere else. It should give us pause that such a posturing for truth is the destructive tendency of much of the right wing. But it is equally the case among self-styled "liberals" who squeeze the scars of truth into universal myths and other flattening schemes. Against that, only the narrative has its liberating say. That is why we must continue to tell these stories and to stay close to the persons who generate them.

In these four analyses I will take up, in turn, four modes of "truth" concerning David. Each concerns a particular literature, reflecting a social context and a social hope, each making a particular theological claim. My analysis is concerned with the convergence of *social context*, *literary articulation*, and *theological claim*, for none of the three will stand without the other two. The theological claim is intimately linked to the literary presentation, but both that claim and that articulation are reflective of and in the service of a certain social world. These various portrayals of David do not live in a vacuum, but are a proposed reading of reality from a certain angle of vision. Nor do these various portrayals easily cohere. But when taken together, they function in a mutually corrective way, so that all these portrayals are needed to present the full reading of David made in the tradition. Any one of us as listeners to this memory may prefer one offer of truth to another. But we must try to hear them all if we would hear the full voice of memory.

The four presentations considered then are:

The Trustful Truth of the Tribe: 1 Sam. 16:1—2 Sam. 5:5 (chap. 1)

The Painful Truth of the Man: 2 Samuel 8—20 and 1 Kings 1—2 (chap. 2)

The Sure Truth of the State: 2 Sam. 5:6—8:18 (chap. 3)

The Hopeful Truth of the Assembly: Psalms 89; 132; Lam. 3:21-27; Isa. 55:3; 1 Chronicles 10—29 (chap. 4)

Hopefully these expositions will illuminate the truth claims of the Bible. Along the way, they may help us also to learn something of the vexed, odd truth about ourselves.

1

THE TRUSTFUL TRUTH
OF THE TRIBE

(1 SAMUEL 16:1—2 SAMUEL 5:5)

THE FIRST OFFER of truth we will consider is the story of how David first appears as a nobody in the narrative of Israel. By the end of this story, David is fully established on the throne. The story is a study of how this nobody becomes the key figure in the life and memory of Israel. For good reason this narrative is conventionally referred to by scholars as "The Rise of David." Here David is on the rise, and we may believe that the community which treasured this portrayal of David cherished his rise, for in it they saw the possibility that they also might rise to social power and social access. And wherever this narrative is rightly practiced, it makes available that same hope that the story of David may become the story of all the others who yearn also to rise.

THE RISE OF DAVID

The beginning point in 1 Sam. 16:1 is clear, because it is there that David appears in the narrative life of Israel for the first time. Moreover, the narrative of 1 Sam. 16:1–13 seems to be peculiarly placed to make an artistic beginning.[1] But the ending is less clear, though many would end this narrative at 2 Sam. 5:5 with David well established as king over Judah and Israel.[2] The narrative is commonly thought to contain a number of independent and very old pieces, but these have now been organized together into a quite intentional narrative that reports on David's move from a nobody to a royal somebody. The interplay of old narrative and intentionality is our main interest. That intentionality has been variously characterized. One scholar sees it as a statement of legitimation for this man and dynasty.[3] Another sees it as an apology.[4] And yet another sees it as glorification and propaganda.[5] It will be observed that all of these judgments move in the same direction: they see the narrative as having an intentional purpose, concerning itself with a major political transition which required this literary justification, and focusing on the person of David. Now if we take all these labels of intentionality—legitimation, apology, glorification, and propaganda—it is clear that we do not have a descriptive account of what happened, nor do we have a critical account that means to balance evidence and assess the data for accuracy. Rather, what we have (all are agreed) is an uncritical narrative which on the one hand is naively enthusiastic for David and on the other hand is relentlessly polemical against Saul. This narrative is not disinterested. Its telling and retelling must pay attention to the vested interest for which the narrative was articulated.

I have characterized this narrative as *the trustful truth of the tribe*. Such a theme indicates not only why it was told, but how it was heard. It also indicates how it must be told and heard now if we are to honor it and take it seriously. This thematic title for the narrative contains three clues:

First, the story is the *truth*. It is not the whole truth, nor objective truth, but it is, for this community, our truth, the discernment of reality on which we are prepared to stake a great deal of life and sacred honor. Every storyteller in the moment of the telling must believe the truth of the story, must for that moment suspend disbelief. That undoubtedly happens here, each time in the retelling. No matter how much of it is imaginative reconstruction, as we have already conceded, the tellers and the listeners must in this moment take the narrative at face value.

Second, I have called it *trustful truth*, that is, it is naive and precritical. This narrative does not notice David's affronts, or if noticed, celebrates them. The story is focused completely on the worth, courage, and destiny of David. The narrative has no critical distance from David to view him either objectively or as an outsider might. It is unambiguously celebrative of him and in that sense I call it trustful. It is incapable of noticing or reporting or objecting to anything critically or negatively.

Having said that, we should notice that the glorification is of a certain kind, even if we use the words "worth," "courage," "virtue." David is not "cleaned up" in the sense that he is innocent, respectable, or puritanical. The virtues valued here are not those of social gentility nor courtly propriety. The David who meets us here is cunning, mocking, and self-serving. He has a kind of animal magnetism, toward both men and women, and things are left raw for imagination. He is not above murder and confiscation of women married to other men, if things fall out that way. He is willing to seize holy bread for survival. So there is narrated here a buoyant, charismatic quality that does not censure, but trustfully celebrates what in other contexts might be an embarrassment.

Third, and finally, we may ask why is this? Here we may ask questions of social criticism and social function. Who would value such a text? Who would experience reality in this way and find it credible? I have called this *the truth of the tribe*. I use "tribe" in Norman K. Gottwald's sense[6]—a unit of society standing apart from and over against the regimentation and legitimation of the state. I do not mean simply rustic, ethnic prestate communities, but units of the marginal who are cast into the marginal role by social necessity and social coercion, who do not have access to the wealth and power of the state and who tend therefore to be irreverent to the civilities of the state.[7] Such communities, without great intentionality, tend to be counter-cultural. And it is for that reason that David might appear to John McKenzie as a bandit and to Niels Peter Lemche[8] as a Habiru (the sociologically marginal). In commenting on the social situation of the Habiru, George Mendenhall writes:

> The clearest example is David. He lost status in the Israelite community by flight caused by the enmity of the king. There gathered about him other refugees motivated by economic as well as other concerns. All were similarly without legal protection and had to maintain themselves by forming a band under the leadership of David, which was then able to survive by cleverness combined with a considerable degree of mobility.[9]

In his discussion of order and vengeance,[10] Mendenhall refers specifically to the episodes of 1 Sam. 24:8–15; 26:10–24,[11] featuring David and his company as enemies of the king and the established civil order. Thus, *this is survival literature*, shaped and told among those who survived by imagination, unsanctioned by the powers of the day. This kind of tribe or tribal grouping must distance itself from the rationality, truth claims, and memories of the dominant state if it is to survive. That is, it must develop its own truth which is cast as a counter-truth.[12] It must be very sure of itself and admit no self-doubt. Now when I term this literature the "trustful truth of the tribe," I mean to understand it as an alternative sketching of reality that serves the interests of a community in deep tension with the dominant rulers and rules of the day. If such a "truth literature" is to provide energy, nerve, and legitimacy for this marginal community, it must of necessity be nervy, unashamed, and a bit bawdy, because it means to provide an alternative world in which to live. This political, partisan narrative of tribal truth is focused on the awesome person of David, who embodied the very elements required for survival. This literature knows, without ever needing to be explicit, that survival requires acting against the civilities of the day, for civilities are modes of social control. To maintain life in a contrasting mode requires distancing from such forms of control. The presence of such literature in the biblical canon must give pause to those of us who have thrived on civility and have come to equate propriety with the claims of faith.

We may note one complicating factor. David is indeed the renegade who attracts other renegades and "nonpersons" to himself. His movement thus is politically doubtful and surely subversive. If he had contented himself with that, a fine story would have been possible. But the outsider yearns for legitimacy, wants that "my truth" should become "the truth."[13] And in this case, David the outsider without any claim moves quickly and relentlessly to the throne and to the social legitimacy that of course goes with it. The Habiru becomes the king (*melek*). The narrative, therefore, does not simply present and sustain an alternative truth. It traces the shrewd moves by which this alternative tribal truth becomes the route to the throne, so that the bandit becomes the new authority. The erstwhile bandit is now the ruler of the day.

We see that tribal truth is expansive here. It is not content to stay tribal. It breaks off in 2 Samuel 5 just at the difficult point where the David story has become the new truth of the state. That is the point of ending and for very good reason. When David has become not only legitimate but the legitimator, it is a very different story which requires a different truth. There is good social and literary reason why the tribal narrative must stop where it does.

To the extent that this narrative seeks to legitimate David (so Artur Weiser and Kyle McCarter), it not only traces the rise of the man. It legitimates this community of tribal truth as well, which now has drawn very close to real power. The narrative thus not only reports an alternative social reality, but it narrates the transformative moves whereby this illegitimate one becomes the authorizer, and creates a new social rationality. All those who may have looked askance at this bandit must come to share this narrative and get inside this world of memory and magnetism if they wish to be insiders. The narrative thus is not simply about the person of David, but about the entire company of those who did not doubt that this one was the wave of God's future. The earlier one joins up, the more fully is this "our truth." The ones who were with David at the start claim and embrace this truth most intensely and unambiguously.

One may then understand this narrative to be hopeful, because it tells, generation after generation, that the marginal ones can become the legitimate holders of power. David is told and retold as a paradigm for all those who yearn for such social transformation. David is a model for the last becoming first, and the story should only be told when we intend to make that subversive claim.

I propose to consider in some detail three episodes of this trustful truth of the tribe. It is obvious that what I have said stands or falls on the concreteness of the text. As we proceed, we ask not only about the *substance* of the narrative, but about its *social function*. What does it do, or intend to do, for those who tell and those who listen? What kind of literary finesse is proper to achieve that social function?

THE INTRODUCTION OF DAVID

The Lord said to Samuel, "How long will you grieve over Saul, seeing I have rejected him from being king over Israel. Fill your horn with oil, and go; I will send you to Jesse the Bethlehemite, for I have provided for myself a king among his sons." And Samuel said, "How can I go? If Saul hears it, he will kill me." And the Lord said, "Take a heifer with you, and say, 'I have come to sacrifice to the Lord.' And invite Jesse to the sacrifice, and I will show you what you shall do; and you shall anoint for me him whom I name to you." Samuel did what the Lord commanded, and came to Bethlehem. The elders of the city came to meet him trembling, and said, "Do you come peaceably?" And he said, "Peaceably; I have come to sacrifice to the Lord; consecrate yourselves, and come with me to the sacrifice." And he consecrated Jesse and his sons, and invited them to the sacrifice.

When they came, he looked on Eliab and thought, "Surely the Lord's anointed is before him." But the Lord said to Samuel, "Do not look on his appearance or on the height of his stature, because I have rejected him; for the Lord sees not as man sees; man looks on the outward appearance, but the Lord looks on the heart." Then Jesse called Abinadab, and made him pass before Samuel. And he said, "Neither has the Lord chosen this one." Then Jesse made Shammah pass by. And he said, "Neither has the Lord chosen this one." And Jesse made seven of his sons pass before Samuel. And Samuel said to Jesse, "The Lord has not chosen these." And Samuel said to Jesse, "Are all your sons here?" And he said, "There remains yet the youngest, but behold, he is keeping the sheep." And Samuel said to Jesse, "Send and fetch him; for we will not sit down till he comes here." And he sent, and brought him in. Now he was ruddy, and had beautiful eyes, and was handsome. And the Lord said, "Arise, anoint him; for this is he." Then Samuel took the horn of oil, and anointed him in the midst of his brothers; and the Spirit of the Lord came mightily upon David from that day forward. And Samuel rose up, and went to Ramah.

1 Samuel 16:1–13

This is the beginning of our narrative.[14] It is the first mention of David, his introduction into the world of the story. So one can imagine that this is done intentionally and carefully. In handling such a narrative, it is most helpful to locate the scenes—not the content points, but the dramatic points—because the truth of the tribe is always dramatic. The scenes are identified when different people are on stage. If the basic structure of the scene is clear—that is, if we know who is on stage and we know what, in that scene, is to serve the larger drama— we may have great freedom and imagination in the actual telling. As long as the scene faithfully serves the larger drama of this move to legitimacy, then it may function as it chooses. Each time it is told, the telling and the context permit it to do something in the community which listens.

Scene I, 16:1–3

This is a scene before the narrative actually begins. No one else in this narrative is privy to this scene. If they were it would spoil everything. The tribal story begins in a secret not generally known, and certainly not known in the big house of the old order. We listeners get in on the secret by overhearing it, but nobody else does, not David, not Saul, not Jesse, only us—and Samuel and Yahweh. It is an interaction of Yahweh and Samuel, and Yahweh is reckoned as a full member of the drama, but not more. The two of them have a lot of private, secret interaction, perhaps a "messianic secret." There is Samuel who is powerful but also increasingly cantankerous, because he seems unable to manage, and that makes one cantankerous. More startling for us is the narrative simplicity of Yahweh. There is no preparation. He just speaks. No apology for such directness, as though the narrator did not notice it is abrupt. Yahweh just speaks. There is no intellectual awkwardness about a God who speaks.

The scene moves to center stage quickly. The pattern is a b á—that is, Yahweh speaks, Samuel speaks, Yahweh speaks. Inside the scene, it is most useful to note the speech pattern. Yahweh's initial speech in v. 1 is in two parts—first a rebuke to Samuel: "We have things to do, you cannot just sit around and sulk" (cf. 2 Sam. 19:5–7). And incidentally (not a major point, but as a supportive aside) we are told that Saul is rejected. That is the premise and problem of the present narrative. That is what this secret community of storytelling knows and celebrates, for this story comes from those who have not had access to power and possessions under Saul. The narrative begins afresh because now there is a chance for a new power configuration. Samuel may be feared and viewed as a crusty man of faith in Israel, but in Yahweh's presence he is on the receiving end.

The second part is a command. That is how Yahweh talks: "fill/go/send." Not much is left open. The command includes a slight rebuke: "I will provide myself a king.[15] I let you do it previously with Saul and you got a loser. So I will do it myself and get it right. Indeed, I have already done it. It is settled." So rebuke and command give the tone. That is how tribal truth begins. Yahweh makes the first move.

Samuel speaks here only once and then briefly. He expresses his fear, for he knows he is sent on a subversive mission. His creature, Saul, is now out of his control. To anoint a counter-king is treasonable, and it will not help to say, "Yahweh sent me." Samuel is not now the brusque man of faith. Now he is an old man staggering under cowardice. Yahweh's answer seems to be prepared in advance. "Good grief, man, lie a little. Tell them something to divert their attention." This Yahweh is not committed to the moral civility of entrenched order. That advice must be good enough, because Samuel's fear is not mentioned again. The scene closes, focused not on the fear of Samuel, but on the command of Yahweh: "You shall anoint for me, whom I name to you." ("You do it—but know it is my act.") The first scene fixes authority. Tribal roots go deep. No political necessity or scheme here. It is all Yahweh's overriding purpose, all preordained. The tribe cannot appeal to reasons of state, but must be grounded more decisively. So the beginning makes tribal truth secret, subversive, uncompromising, rooted in the action of God alone, beyond scrutiny.

Scene II, 16:4–5

This narrative element concerns only a small matter. Perhaps it is included only to indicate how ominous the journey of Samuel is for all parties. There is less speech here, more narrative. First, Samuel is obedient. Within the confines of the narrative he has no choice. Second, the elders of the city (Bethlehem) are trembling. They want to know why he comes. They do not even know yet whose side he is on. They presume he is still an agent of Saul. If so, the Judeans tremble because Saul is no friend of southerners. Or if he is not an agent of Saul, it is even more dangerous, because then he may come to include them in an act of betrayal, which is more risk than they want. After all, villagers do not much care which overlord exploits them. Mostly they hope not to be noticed. In any case, the entry of Samuel is not routine. His very coming is a harbinger of something unsettled and dangerous.

"Oh," he says (just as Yahweh had told him to say in v. 2; cf. Luke

19:31), "I come to offer a sacrifice." So he implements the ruse, as Yahweh had instructed. The second scene does not advance the story significantly. In relation to what follows, it moves from the more general (elders) to the less general (Jesse), to the specific target (David). It serves a dramatic function—to heighten the suspense.

Scene III, 16:6–10

The tribes delight in telling this episode. It warns against looking on appearance, because the monied, landed people tend also to be the beautiful people. This is the procession through which Samuel reviews the available sons of Jesse. There are two dramas going on at the same time in this scene: one that the players see, one that is hidden between Yahweh and Samuel, as in scene I. Again, as the listeners we share the secret denied the players.

In the public scene there are seven sons passed in review. It had to be seven sons (cf. Job 1:2). In good narrative fashion three are named, Eliab, Abinadab, Shammah. When the pattern is three times established, the other four are presented in a quick, undeveloped summary. Eliab is impressive and Samuel is seduced by his appearance. And so also by the other six. The scene is quickly spent. It yields nothing. There must have been eagerness in the family, knowing they are under consideration. Then there is dismay, for after seven sons, the entire stable of would-be kings is exhausted.

In the secret drama going on all the while, Samuel listens and does not speak. As in scene I, he is again rebuked by Yahweh: "Do not look on appearances." It is a scolding earned by the selection of Saul. Samuel had picked the first one, judging by appearances (1 Sam. 9:2). He did not work. Two things happen here. "First," says Yahweh, "do not make the same mistake a second time. Second, just so you do not, I will pick this time." This is Yahweh's own, direct, personal choice. The tribe knows! God alone did this for David.

In a second way, scene III repeats themes of scene I, by repetition of the word "reject." Saul was rejected. Now Eliab the oldest son is also rejected. Both are of good appearance. Both are rejected. Because Yahweh looks on the heart. He waits for the weak eighth son, the unnoticed one, who has a good heart.

Publicly, scene III is a failure and yields nothing. In hidden terms scene III is important but preliminary. It knows that this is not a failure, but a waiting. The trustful tribe knows in hearing the story again. This is not the end. There is a fourth scene. Jesse, and even Samuel, do not know that yet. But we do, we who listen as the trusting tribe. This third scene pivots on the terms "reject/choose" (*mā'as/bāḥar*) with *baḥar* used three times in the negative. In this scene there is only rejection: "not choose, not choose, not choose." The choosing waits for the next surprising move.

We may pause over the motif of "reject/choose," as even the trustful tribe paused. We have had some important rejections here. We have had the legitimated king rejected. We have had the oldest son rejected, one of the beautiful people. That is politically important to the tribe, if the tribe be understood as the assemblage of the marginal. The powerful and the beautiful are always chosen, not us. It is nice to have a tale in which the usually chosen son is rejected. This narrative works critically and knowingly against that common practice. When there is the next choosing, it will be "one of us," one of the uncredentialed nobodies. Already there is the sense that God chose what is lowly and despised in the world to bring to nought the things that are (1 Cor. 1:26–31). This is a nobody of an eighth son!

Scene IV, 16:11–13

If this had been a narrative of rejection, it could have ended in v. 10. Yahweh has not chosen. But the tribe does not tell the story in order for it to end in rejection. The tribe consists of those who have waited a long time. Now the tribe waits for a choosing of one of their own. And so there is a fourth scene. It opens with a question by Samuel. He has been rebuked twice, but he is firmly under orders. He asks, "Are all your sons here?" He asks the question almost fearfully. Is the promise in vain? Is the risky, treasonable trip to Bethlehem wasted? On the one hand, he hopes there is another to make the trip and the risk all worthwhile. On the other hand, it would be simple and un-complicated if there were no other, for then he is clean. But he gets a positive answer. There is one more, one after the perfect seven. This one is young, insignificant, keeping sheep.

Now the tribe listens eagerly—one more time—for the next dra-matic move. One of ours, one of the very lowly, marginal ones is about to enter the narrative and change everything. Keep your eye on him. Samuel speaks tersely, perhaps against his own better judgment. "Bring him, we will not sit down till then."

The remainder of the episode quickly unravels. Yahweh commissions: "This is he—anoint him." We have come to the treasonable payoff for the journey. Samuel obeys promptly. He does not even comment, as he characteristically does about everything.

The wind rushes on David. The lowly one is seized by the Spirit. Samuel heads home, mission accomplished, now an implicated accomplice. But the tribe understands. The wind rushes on the lowly. Now they are equal to all the powerful who have everything but the wind.

One peculiar note the narrative cannot resist. We have been put on notice in 16:7: Do not look on appearance, look on the heart. But a wistful aside is offered in v. 12. This eighth son is impressive: He is ruddy, has beautiful eyes, is handsome. But of course that is not why he is chosen. But one cannot help but notice. And noticing, one cannot help but comment. Perhaps in that moment of recognition are sown some seeds of what is to come later. He was a choice made only on the grounds of *fidelity*. But what a man! One need not deny the power of *virility*. Virility just drips off of him. The people in the big house do not possess all the manhood that is available. It makes one wonder if that is a factor in his being anointed. One cannot tell the relation between the act of anointing and this observation. Is he anointed finally because he looks the part, and is Samuel one more time deceived? Or is he anointed in spite of all of that, because an eighth son has a different heart? We are not told. But the Spirit does not hesitate. It comes mightily. In that moment history is turned. The tribe knows and applauds. Obviously a very special narrative is the beginning point. The narrative is enveloped in 16:1 by the break with the past carried in the word "reject," and by the rush of the Spirit in v. 13. That statement gives an anticipation of what is to come. Yahweh has the last word as well as the first word. In v. 6 Samuel picks a candidate, but in v. 12 Yahweh designates the real king, a candidate different from the one Samuel would have picked. Samuel is wrong. Yahweh has seen his own king. Not even Saul can be credited. Samuel, left to his own judgment, would have missed again.

The narrative can be termed propaganda, but I think it is better regarded as pre-propaganda. It is more a yearning, not calculating enough, more amazed about how this beginning is made against all odds and against all conventional expectations. David is indeed *ex nihilo*, and the tribes rally around him. Of course, the narrative is not historical in the sense of factual reportage. But it is "history making." It is a narrative that creates a world for the marginal ones.[16] What they sense in David is that real power is not in the forms seen by human eyes, but in the wind that is not seen, yet irresistible. As the wind blows where it will (John 3:8), it is not administered by the old agencies of governance that have served only to monopolize for some and exclude others. This is narrative from the other side, from below. It proposes a world alternative to the one of monopoly and exclusion. Such a telling gives the tribe someone in whom to have hope, someone in whom to trust in dangerous and unreserved ways.

DAVID AND GOLIATH

1 Samuel 17

This long narrative is the entire account of the encounter of David and Goliath. There are two problems in our treatment of it. The first is a practical problem. It is too long to review in detail, and it is too well known. The second problem is a critical one. There is a great confusion about who in fact killed Goliath, though most think it was not David.[17] This narrative is judged to be rather late in the building of the tradition,[18] but we will deal with it in its present location. Let me suggest the tribal reading of this true narrative. (Clearly I do not regard "tribal" narration as necessarily early. The delineation has to do with social function, not chronology.)

The actual battle between the two forces is brief. It takes exactly two verses (1 Sam. 17:48–49). David ran quickly, took a stone, slung it, struck Goliath. He fell. That is the whole tale. That is the core reference which must have been the root of the long dramatic narrative that now clusters around it. Whatever critical judgments may be made, the truth of the tribe assigns this victory irretrievably to David. David is celebrated as the champion against the overlords and all else serves the celebration. This is not simply a romance of a little boy against a giant. It is a much larger struggle of the marginal against the tyrants. And every marginal community can join the truth of this tribe. (No doubt that is why children like the story and rally around it, because they also live in a world of oppressive giants.)

The narrative does not rush along. First we observe that it takes a long time to set the stage, in 1 Sam. 17 1–30. Four times the narrative introduces a new character in the drama. This seems to be done with great discipline and intentionality, almost as if the narrator were introducing the cast:

Verse 1: "Now the Philistines gathered their armies for battle." That is enough to create fear. The ante is upped in v. 4 with a detailed characterization of Goliath. Note that the narrative is much more interested here in characterization than in action (vv. 4–7):

And there came out from the camp of the Philistines a champion named Goliath, of Gath, whose height was six cubits and a span. He had a helmet of bronze on his head, and he was armed with a coat of mail, and the weight of his coat was five thousand shekels of bronze. And he had greaves of bronze upon his legs, and a javelin of bronze slung between his shoulders. And the shaft of his spear was like a weaver's beam, and his spear's head weighed six hundred shekels of iron; and his shield-bearer went before him.

That description takes four verses, compared to only two for the killing. The narrator lingers to be sure that the tribe understands the odds and therefore the terror.

Verses 12 and 14 indicate that David was the eighth son of Jesse. Not much could be expected. He is still an outsider. He is still doing menial chores. All he gets to do here is to carry the lunch boxes of his brave brothers. The introduction of David is in sharp contrast to that of Goliath. The contrast serves the surprise in the action to come.

Verse 19: "Now Saul, . . . and all the men of Israel, were in the valley of Elah, fighting with the Philistines." They are not described, however, as doing anything but fighting. They, in fact, do nothing. They are immobilized in their fear. Perhaps they are waiting for a miracle. They are realistic enough not to hope. They could think of nothing to do, except to talk with each other about how terrible it all was. Their talk generated more fear. It is the way of the oppressor not to control by violence but by intimidation. The Philistines did not need to do much but "to flex their muscles," and the tribes quaked and knuckled under. They could imagine no alternative.

Verse 28: Now Eliab, David's eldest brother, is angry. We have heard of him before. He was Samuel's candidate for king. He is said to be angry. At least he is able to care and have passion. But his anger is not against the passive Israelites as it might have been, or against the intimidating Philistines as it could have been. No, he is angry with little David. Well, of course. Little brothers bother big brothers, especially if big brothers are pretending to be mighty men of valor— who are immobilized in fear and cannot fight. David's presence immediately exposes Eliab as a coward, and all the men with him. But we also know he is rejected. He is all dressed up, but in the drama that he is still unable to see, he has nowhere to go. The tribe will never be free as long as it plays by the rules of the oppressor and lets that definition of reality prevail. That is what the armies of Saul have done. They are hopeless, already co-opted before the battle was under way.

Now the scene is set with all the principal parties in place:

Goliath, armed to the teeth, embodiment of all that is fierce and terrifying about the Philistines.

David, an innocent little boy; at the most, an undesirable intrusion.

Saul, an immobilized, terrified king, who has yielded everything to the enemy in defining the world.

Eliab, an angry, rejected, rejecting older brother.

The narrator skillfully refrains from tipping his hand concerning the development of this interplay.

In 1 Sam. 17:31–40, the denouement draws closer, in an exchange between Saul, the one compromised and immobilized, and David, the unwelcome innocent. The narrative again makes a sweeping characterization, careful to give us the details sufficient to make the point.

First, there is an exchange in vv. 31–37 which culminates in the passionate speech of David (vv. 34–37). David must have loved the speech on his tongue, knowing that he had been called and created to make this very speech. For the marginal tribes, this speech must have been a treasured memory, for this is raw power and courage outside authorized channels. In vv. 34–36, the speech concerns personal bravery. Only in v. 37 does the speech of David make a theological acknowledgment: "The Lord who delivered me from the paw of the lion and from the paw of the bear, will deliver me from this Philistine." Indeed, Goliath will be easy after a bear or a lion. Notice the speech does not refer to a specific lion or bear, but makes a grand general claim about David's characteristic power. Against such as these[19] David saves the helpless: "the lamb." I delivered, I caught, I smote, I killed. David is the only one in camp who is capable of such action verbs. All of it points to the lamb. Does the narrative know something in anticipation of Nathan's parable in 2 Sam. 12:1–5? Or perhaps Nathan remembers this claim. Here David attends to the lambs, playing the role of "savior" (cf. Isa. 40:9–11). In 2 Samuel 11—12, he is the "predator." But that is a different offer of truth and does not belong to the tribe.

In 17:37, the dynamics are inverted. David who delivers will be delivered. David who snatches from lions will be snatched to safety by Yahweh. This reference to Yahweh (Lord) is the first in the narrative. The name has been withheld as long as possible. One might have expected the king or even the taunting enemy to use the name of Yahweh. But the word is held for the only one who believes in this God who saves slaves, as the one who cares for and keeps the lambs. It is David who in v. 26 alludes to the God of Israel as "the living God." But even there he does not name God. He only characterizes him. So the narrative holds the key name until the proper moment. The utterance of the name in v. 37 convinces Saul, who now repeats the name, gives a blessing and his royal sanction: "Go, and the Lord be with you." The narrative anticipates that David must triumph on two fronts, both against the Philistines and against Saul. Saul is the trickier enemy, but already here his defeat is under way.

After the royal permit, the narrative again carefully builds the case by description. Saul does not understand anything. He has uttered Yahweh's name. But he wants to outdo Goliath on Goliath's terms in vv. 38–39. So he offers armor, helmet, coat of mail, sword—David "tried in vain to go" with such encumbrance. David's contrast is with both Saul and Goliath. Unlike them, he goes unencumbered ("I am not used to them"). Both of them—the one a braggart, the other a coward—trust in arms. But David does not trust in arms, because of who he is and because of who his people are, people who have learned that the others always have a monopoly of arms.[20] The tribe must fight in another way. David takes five smooth stones and his sling. They are enough.

After the exchange with Saul which tested David considerably, we finally have the encounter in 1 Sam. 17:41–47. But again the talk is more interesting than the actual fight. First, Goliath speaks (vv. 43–44)—a haughty put-down. Then David (vv. 45–47) makes his eloquent speech, a match for his speech in vv. 34–37. David contrasts the conventional way of sword/spear/javelin—the way trusted by both Goliath and Saul—with his own covenantal way, in the name of the Lord of the troops (vv. 46–47):

> This day the Lord will deliver you into my hand, and I will strike you down, and cut off your head; and I will give the dead bodies of the host of the Philistines this day to the birds of the air and to the wild beasts of the earth; that all the earth may know that there is a God in Israel, and that all this assembly may know that the Lord saves not with sword and spear; for the battle is the Lord's and he will give you into our hand.[21]

The argument is not one of pacifism, but is an argument that lives in the context of the technology and equipment available to the tribe, which is not the same as the established powers. The equalizer is Yahweh who is among the tribes, not among the established powers.

The battle follows quickly (vv. 48–49). So also the rout of the Philistines (vv. 50–53). Finally David has formal access to Saul and to royal power (vv. 55–58). Here the narrative slows to a deliberate pace after the feverish action (v. 58): "And Saul said to him, 'Whose son are you, young man?' And David answered, 'I am the son of your servant Jesse the Bethlehemite.'" Note well, his name is still not disclosed. He does not tell Saul his name and he does not rush to put himself in Saul's power or at Saul's disposal. One does not do that in survival literature. It appears that he maintains his freedom and withholds himself from the king's power.

The story has a transparent impact. We do not need to linger. But we make four observations:

1. The contrast of David and all the others—Goliath, Saul, Eliab—is clear. What emerges is not only a contrast, but a singular focus on David at the expense of all the others. He is seen to be a "maker of

history." That is, he acts in ways that give a new future to his community.

2. The speeches dominate the narrative. The two speeches of David are decisive. One is to Saul (vv. 34–37), the other to Goliath (vv. 45–47). This is of crucial importance for biblical faith, but especially for the tribal trajectory. What people say goes far to determine which world they will live in. That lets us see the imaginative power of the storyteller who constructs what should have been said and therefore what world is legitimately embraced. David's speeches are marked with a vitality appropriate to his character, and even more to the marginal community that trusts in him.

3. The speeches of David, in both cases, point *beyond* David *to* Yahweh. In both speeches it is the deliverance of Yahweh that matters. David, as well as Goliath, is set in the perspective of this reference and defined by it. The narrative ends with the assembly not being in doubt that there is a God in Israel. And Israel knows.

4. Now we hazard one other point. Both David the deliverer and Yahweh the deliverer belong with the tribe. Here David is not a palace man but a nobody. At this point Yahweh is not yet accommodated, but is still the God of the liberated tribes.[22] The story in its dramatic telling and in its theological claims resonates precisely with those who draw close to a liberation against all the oppressors. They are the ones who yet believe there is a living God who is not intimidated or immobilized by swords and coats of mail and bombastic speech. Thus Yahweh is unlike the armies of Saul who are intimidated and immobilized. This liberated God is drawn to the marginal ones of the tribe. They wait to be snatched like a lamb from the mouth of the lion.

SAUL AND DAVID

1 Samuel 24[23]

Throughout this literature, the Philistines are a perennial threat. That is part of the social reality that makes this tribal existence precarious. But alongside the Philistines, there is Saul and the movement in Israel toward monarchial consolidation. Of the two, the intense interaction with the Saul movement is more important. This has been so since the beginning in 1 Sam. 16:1–13, the tension between the rejected and the chosen. Will David win over Saul? Will the south prevail over the north? Will the free tribal leader defeat the established power? These are more than theoretical questions, for those who staked their lives on David have everything at issue. The narrative deals with large issues concerning the social conflict, but is so beholden to David that everything is personalized, and filtered through his presence.

In 1 Samuel 24, vv. 1–7 describe the main action. The remainder of the chapter consists of two speeches exploring the implications of the action. The action is simple enough. David is rightly perceived as a threat. Of course, it is all told from David's perspective. Perhaps among the partisans of Saul this is only a necessary police action against subversion at the fringe. So Saul sets out with three thousand men to get David. Fair enough. But the story turns on this intimate detail. We imagine we are dealing with a great public conflict, but instead what we get is what happens to the king while he is squatting to defecate.[24] Saul stops at a cave "to relieve himself" (v. 3). Is this mockery in the tribal telling? The great king, from whom the Spirit has now departed, is seen at his most vulnerable.

The narrator wants us to sense the inscrutability of the events. Who would have believed he stopped at the very cave in which David was resting? The drama quickens. We should not miss the unavoidable conclusion that the entire episode is indeed providential.

David is egged on by his men. This is the moment for which they have been waiting. David goes halfway with them. He will not commit an act of violence, but he will leave his calling card in an unmistakable symbolic gesture. He cuts off "the skirt of Saul's robe" (v. 4). Gunn suggests the word used, *kanap*, is deliberately a euphemism for sexual organ, a sexual extremity that could have been cut off as easily as the robe. In any case, this is how close David is to Saul. That is how "exposed" Saul is to David. Was the cave that dark? The narrator knows only so much. He knows that David immediately regretted the action (v. 5), for he had humiliated the king by exploiting his vulnerability. The narrative reads as though David intended to act without restraint, but stopped out of his self-serving commitment to the royal office.

The narrator renders David marvelously ambiguous. Is this deference genuine? Is it a ploy? Certainly it is calculating. We are not told enough to know for sure. But that is necessary to survival literature. The truth for tribes must always be a bit open and inscrutable in the face of other truths which always know too much. Obviously the restraint shown here is of a quality not unlike that of Jesus before Pilate. If one acts too decisively, one will be wrong—and dead.

1 Samuel 24 includes an extended speech by David (vv. 8–15). The narrative is mostly people talking to each other. This speech is grandly self-serving and ingratiating. But the speech also has a streak of nobility, a tough and uncompromising nobility that puts David completely in the right and leaves Saul in a morally and politically exposed position. In 24:10 David points out that Saul was at his disposal, but he did not dispose of him because he is the Lord's anointed. While David may treat the person of Saul with considerable contempt, he respects the office, no doubt with an eye on soon occupying it himself. That verse addressed things formally in respect to the king. In 24:11 the tone changes with the address, "My father," and the tone becomes much more personal and intimate. But the same point is made: David had a chance to kill and did not take it. Verses 12–16 are a tightly woven statement. Verse 12 begins, "May the Lord judge between me and you." And it ends in v. 15 with the same formula somewhat intensified, "May the Lord therefore be judge and give sentence between me and you." This is capped by an appeal that Yahweh plead the cause of David and deliver him from the hand of Saul, even as in v. 10 Saul has been delivered from the hand of David. Between the two juridical formulas, David quotes a proverb—"out of the wicked comes forth wickedness" (v. 13)—which in fact asserts his own innocence, and by implication, the guilt of Saul. Then in v. 14 he uses rhetorical questions as a way of deflating Saul even further. The speech is an extraordinary rhetorical flourish, a tribal articulation not only of David's innocence but of David's shrewd capacity to make his way and to beat the enemies of the movement. The political effect of the speech is served by the literary, rhetorical way of the words.

Saul's speech in response (24:16–22) is an argument that could only come from the tribe. Saul concedes everything to David, because the narrative knows better than Saul or David where all of this is headed. The future that is here offered is a future in which David has triumphed completely. Saul is dismissed as a guilty failure and the heirs of Saul

are empty-handed suppliants. It is conceded that David is innocent—
"you are more righteous than I." He does not practice vengeance, so
the statement says, but he does good to his enemy. Verse 19 affirms
that David has acted in a most unusual way, for normally a person will
not treat an enemy so. In the words of Saul, the transference of royal
power from Saul to David is anticipated: "I know that you shall surely
be king, and that the kingdom of Israel shall be established in your
hand" (24:20). This moment marks the actual, literary moment of trans-
fer, even though it takes political events a while to catch up to the
literary reality presented here.

Saul is here contrasted sharply with David. He opens the conversation with a pleading, faltering question, "Is that you?" Alter[25] suggests
this is an echo of Isaac, "Is that your voice, my son?" The Saul of this
pericope knows the truth. He knows that the current power struggle
is destined to end in David's favor at his own expense, and so he is
properly deferential. In Saul's own mouth is the articulation of his
unavoidably tragic role vis à vis David.

The throne is conceded. It is best to put the concession speech in
the mouth of the loser. Verse 21 adds only a final personal bargaining:
"Swear to me therefore by the Lord that you will not cut off my
descendants after me." David swears and the meeting is ended. As we
watch David subsequently, in other offers of truth, this promise is
shaky at best.

But for now, note how this truth is constructed. One does not know
for sure how to take it, and surely we are not intended by the narrative
to know how to take it. Many things are left marvelously ambiguous.
Is David genuine in his respect for Saul? Does the narrator wink at
the listeners, as we wait for the right moment? We do not know. But
the fact that we have to ask such a critical question means that we are
likely not of the tribe. Because the tribe knows. It is their truth. The
tribe is content to know that David will do the right thing. Indeed,
whatever David does will be the right thing. There is not a word spoken
in criticism of David. It does not matter if he is genuine here or not.
The tribe will wait for its truth to come to fullness. But it will not wait
too long.

Now clearly this is a study in David. But I want you not to miss the
sociological point. This is a practice of tribal truth. Tribal truth comes

early in our sorting things out. Tribal truth is a way of valuing what is closest to us, with passion and power and with uncritical naiveté. One of the awarenesses that comes is that such tribal truth is present in the Bible. We are among those who dare to call it the live Word of God, the only rule for life and faith.

One cannot read this narrative discerningly without becoming aware of how ambiguous our claim of truth is. It is fortuitous, perhaps lucky, and no doubt tendentious, when we can regard as "the Lord's anointed" the one who also is the leader of our particular tribe, bringing to light our best hopes and advocating our best interests. Such a nice equation of *interest and truth* works through this narrative. One might have wished for a more nearly pure offer of truth about "the Lord's anointed." It would not be such an embarrassment. But this is partisan literature and it is partisan faith. It dares to believe not only that David is a partisan man, but that God is a partisan God and that truth is in some way a party to our hopes and interests. This narrative is not the whole of David's truth, nor is partisanship the whole of our truth. But it is a powerful factor. Its power operates in spite of Samuel who had other ideas, in spite of Goliath who had better arms, in spite of Saul who had better credentials. This narrative is a study of how the wind of God blows in the life of the tribe, not to be administered, but to evoke amazement. And when one is genuinely amazed, one need not be embarrassed at its partisan tendency. The wind of God which gives justice and wholeness and power blows where it wills. This narrative presents a time when the wind blew in the happy direction of this tribe, through this peculiar man.

2

THE PAINFUL TRUTH
OF THE MAN

(2 SAMUEL 9—20 AND 1 KINGS 1—2)

Here we consider a second, very different element
in the story told about David. I will follow the conventional assumption
that there are two great narratives about David. "The Rise of David"
(1 Sam. 16:1—2 Sam. 5:5) is one of these (chap. 1). It is the account
of David moving from the margin to the center of power. The other,
to which we now turn, is called the "Succession Narrative," so named
because it is asked in 1 Kings 1:20, "Who shall sit on the throne after
David?"[1] (Leonard Rost, and many after him, assumed that the narrative is preoccupied with the question of "succession to the throne"
after David, and the narrative reports on the various ways in which
the throne is sought, by battle and by scheme. Although that assumption about the intent of the narrative is increasingly doubted, the title
tends still to be used.)

The conventional assumption is that these are two distinct narratives.
Scholars have given very little attention to the question of their relation
to each other. Two different notions on this matter may be reported.
First, Aage Carlson has suggested that the two conventional narratives
are juxtaposed so that the first portrays David "under blessing" and
the second, David "under curse."[2] While Carlson's proposal has not
received great support, Brevard S. Childs has taken note of it as a way
of proceeding that takes seriously the canonical shape of the literature.[3]

More recently and more delicately, Robert Alter has suggested that
there is no overriding reason to divide the text into these two units,

but it may be quite acceptable to see the literature all of a single piece with one "unified imaginative conception."[4] Alter may be correct on this point, but he has only asserted the matter and has not given it any careful analysis. And even if this is the case, Alter has observed a different and no less important distinction between the two elements which most scholars separate and which Carlson has juxtaposed with theological intentionality. In the former, the "Rise of David," the narrative focuses exclusively and with severe discipline only upon the *public* David, screening out any probe of David's person, attitude, or motive. Alter understands this as a deliberate artistic strategy. Such a strategy fits with my suggestion that the first narrative is the trustful truth of the tribe—truth that is uncritical of David and is unwilling to engage in any speculation or to probe any ambiguity or mixed motive that David may have entertained. The narrative does not want to assess David's interiority, because that may lead to a lessening of nerve.

In the episode of David-Uriah-Bathsheba and the death of the resultant child, however, the narrative turns increasingly to reflect on the *interiority* of David, and all the delicacy, ambiguity, and freedom that David in fact exercises.[5] I find Alter's suggestion rich with possibility. In a rather elusive way, he suggests that it is the shattering effect of a child's death (2 Sam. 12:15–23) that breaks things open and perhaps moves to a disclosure of enormous depth. Death does indeed do that on occasion. It is possible to take it with Alter as a literary strategy. Or it is possible, in Carlson's terms, to suggest that the agenda of David "under curse" necessarily requires a disclosure of the agony and anguish of this failed man. But such a strategy is not necessary, for it would have been possible to chronicle the curse in terms of purely external public affairs, though the narrator has chosen not to.

Alter's suggestion has one very special point in its favor. It is conventional to treat 2 Samuel 9—10 as the beginning of the Succession Narrative, but these two chapters are commonly regarded as preliminary, not very crucial to the narrative, and not very interesting. The real action, according to most interpreters, begins in 2 Samuel 11 with Uriah and Bathsheba. The upshot of Alter's suggestion is that the David-Uriah-Bathsheba episode is lifted up as the key to the entire story. That is, it is the break point for David, though one must mean not a description of a historical break point but a strategy of the narrator in arranging the narrative in this way. It is David's awful moment of self-knowledge when he no longer believes his press notices, and is no longer either able or compelled to be the uncritical public David. The incredible miscalculation (sin?) with Uriah and Bathsheba opens David, according to the narrator, to the awareness of ambiguity of a moral kind. It is the kind of moral ambiguity that the David of the "Rise of David" story could never entertain. And from that shattering moment, the narrator, the community around the story, and perhaps David, are permitted to enter a new world of personal interiority with all its problematic of anguish, ambiguity, ambition, and ambivalence. The public David continues to function, but the public David is no longer able or permitted to override, censor, and ignore the personal David. Now the two are placed in a deep and unresolvable tension.[6]

Alter's suggestion has a great deal of merit. My own judgment is that he may be followed in his discernment of the character and quality of the literature without taking his critical judgment that all the narrative is one unit. I do not follow that judgment because the case still has to be made for it against the critical consensus.

THE MAN DAVID

Let me suggest a variant form of that same sense of narrative intention. I presume that in the Succession Narrative we have a different storyteller. No longer are we dealing here with trustful truth that is incapable of criticism. Now we have a way of truth that looks more closely, if not with suspicion, at least critically and knowingly. It is no longer tribal truth, for this truth is too daring and ambiguous to serve the tribe. David is now ensconced within the palace, like the tribal narrative never knew him to be. He has an army, a bureaucracy, a harem. If anything, he contradicts the hopes and needs of the tribe. A very long time, sociologically if not chronologically, has passed since the tribal truth. This literature is neither tribal nor trustful. I suggest that the reason this narrative takes such a different posture is that it is a different narrative with a different agenda, an agenda that had to present a very different David. The difference, of course, may have been partly in the eye and circumstance of the beholder, but not completely. This surely is a very different David. I will refer to this portrayal of David as "the painful truth of the man."

Think about that phrasing. It is narrative now about a man, perhaps *the* man. Of course the narrative knows this man is the king. That fact is acknowledged, but is not taken too seriously. The narrator is not overly impressed. Rather the narrator cuts through all the royal business to see the man, to see him as an ambiguous, contradictory, enmeshed man, driven and inept, with a range of emotional possibilities. It is the earliest portrayal in Israel of the human creature with such depth and discernment, and it is surely the most imaginative picture we have of David, or of anyone in the Bible.

It could be that the narrative has political interest.[7] Indeed, it would be strange if it did not. And yet what that interest might be is not transparent, for scholars have suggested the narrative is pro-David or anti-David, pro-Solomon or anti-Solomon.[8] If one can argue in all such directions, one may conclude that the author is unclear, that the author is not interested in such questions, or that the author is carefully and cunningly subtle about such dangerous issues. Clearly the narrative is not excessively polemical or apologetic. The narrator keeps an eye on the man, perhaps to let the political chips fall where they will. Now I do not suggest that this is a psychological study of the kind that Erik Erikson might write. This man is a public man and any report cannot disregard his public life. If he were not a public man, he would not be so interesting, nor would things be so difficult. What we have, then, is an intimate portrayal of a public man. We learn the truth about him. It is a truth that cuts underneath tribal truth that tended not to notice such matters. This narrator, in contrast to the tribal presentation, waits more patiently and observes more closely and with more discerning imagination.

That patient wait and that discerning imagination see, finally, a great deal of pain and anguish. That is where the story leads as it takes us inside. The contrast is clear. There is little anguish in the tribal statement we have already considered. There things move quickly and successfully, from triumph to triumph. Even where David troubles about things, it always seems to have calculating political purpose. But not now. Now, in the Succession Narrative, we observe the anguish and trouble of a man whose *personal agenda* and *public role* keep him embroiled in painful ways. So I propose that this narrative of the painful truth of the man be taken for that, a biblical discernment that human personhood, bound as it must be to public history, is always and inevitably a life of anguish. On the one hand, such an insight is a refutation of all modern romanticism that believes and promises that life can be uncomplicated like "I'm O.K., you're O.K." On the other hand, it is a remarkable ancient discernment which argues against all mythic notions that human life does not count for anything and that the gods manage it all. This narrative asserts against both ancient and modern deceptions that human life has freedom and anguish, power and pain, and neither is avoidable for those mirrored in this astonishing man.[9]

We deal here with a man, a public man, a man who happens to be king, a man with enormous power, both technical and official, as well as personal and visceral. But he is nonetheless a man. And if we deal with a man now partially unadorned, we deal with pain, for pain is constitutive of human life. There is more pain here than the tribe noticed, for the tribe is too innocent, too buoyant, too sure to notice. There is more pain here than the state will notice in our next discussion, for the state deals in summaries, and if it is not too cynical, it is at least too unconcerned to notice.

Two more preliminary comments. First, lodged for just a moment between *the ebullience of the tribe* and *the jadedness of the state*, this narrative notices that human life is marked by pathos, by a sense of incongruity, a wistfulness, a lingering regret about all that cannot be recalled. Prior to this literary moment, one might have seen pathos in the Saul narrative, but the text is not empathetic enough with Saul to share the pathos.[10] It must criticize and dismiss. After David, Solomon is not vulnerable enough, does not want to be human enough, is not known enough, for such pathos. Saul has not enough healthful strength for his pitifulness to be valued, and Solomon is not open enough to cause us to linger. I emphasize this point so that we do not miss what a remarkable literary achievement this is.[11] It is a breakthrough whenever a narrative makes this fragile balance that touches the most profound dimensions of humanness. That is possible because of the sensitivity of this narrator. It is also made possible because the subject, David, has such continuing generative power.

The last preliminary point is this. This narrative, which focuses stunningly on this person, does so in a way that lets David become a model or a paradigm for humanness. It is precisely the concreteness, when it rings true, that permits generalization and identification. I have, in another setting, argued that the David of this narrative provides the main clues for understanding the narratives of Genesis 2— 11, and that these primal narratives in part are a generalizing of this story and this man.[12] Thus, I suggest that the narratives in Genesis quite intentionally drew out the insights of this royal interiority. The continuing power of the narrative is that we continue to find ourselves portrayed in this narrative about this pained man. We know it is the truth about him, and about us. The narrative thus becomes not only a probing disclosure, but also a good word spoken against us from the outside, that is, by the narrative.

SHAPE AND TEXTURE OF THE SUCCESSION NARRATIVE

Before turning to a specific text, some general comments are in order concerning the shape and texture of the Succession Narrative. These comments are intended to provide an orientation to some critical understandings, but more particularly to some theological nuances that are present in the text.

First we note that this extended narrative is organized around four primary episodes.[13] Each of these narratives is in itself an extraordinary work of art. They are:

David-Uriah-Bathsheba: 2 Samuel 11—12
Amnon-Tamar-Absalom: 2 Samuel 13—14[14]
Absalom's rebellion: 2 Samuel 15—19[15] (with an addendum in chap. 20)
Solomon's coup: 1 Kings 1—2

Each of these narrative units has been extensively studied. While each constitutes a dramatic unity in its own right, we may consider the linkage between the parts and the impact of the total narrative. I suggest that the David-Uriah-Bathsheba episode lays out the inescapable problematic of the entire narrative. From this moment of hubris, there will be no peace for David or for his family. And that episode with its spinoff in 2 Sam. 12:24–25 bequeaths to us the baby Solomon, whom Yahweh loves, but who is nonetheless the offspring of this royal sordidness. There is here a commitment on God's part to the future, but it is made in a terribly ambiguous situation, perhaps not without embarrassment. That initial commitment to Solomon resurfaces in the conclusion in 1 Kings 1—2. The power of that initial episode is not unlike the power of Genesis 37 in the total Joseph narrative.[16] In the end Solomon manages to take the throne from his brother, the rightful heir. What should we have expected from this son come late to this illicit, ambiguous relationship? Indeed, the sword will never depart from this house (2 Sam. 12:10), and now at the other end of the narrative (1 Kings 1:51; 2:8; 2:23) the rise of Solomon is essentially a mobilization of the sword. The narrator knows it could not be otherwise. So the narrative wants us to remember the beginning as we observe the shameful, shabby conclusion.

The intermediate episodes carry the story line, first the elimination of Amnon (2 Sam. 13:28–29), and then the elimination of Absalom (18:31—19:4). Told from the perspective of Solomon, the story moves in its relentless way to power and success. But lived from David's side, each narrative augments the pain, all triggered by his self-deception at the outset.

Next, one should note that the episodes tend to work at the fine interface of *public responsibility and power*, and *personal temptation and self-deception*. If there had been no interiority to David, if there were only public events, the narrative would scarcely attract us. It is not really news if a king seizes a wife of another man. It is not news if a king kills his son who tries to take the throne from him. It is not news if a king instructs his favorite son in the ways of blood, for the sake of the throne, especially if the king is on his deathbed. Taken as public record, this is not news. We do a disservice if we flatten the story into a report on what happened.

This odd narrative holds our attention precisely because the story-teller has another discernment to offer. The narrator knows that human persons, even kings, are not summaries, but are mysteries that must be taken one at a time and at a slow, reflective pace. This narrator takes us inside David's family, even inside David and inside the interaction between David and David's God. And the main gain here, an advance beyond the first narrative we have considered, is that there is an interiority that is not simple or unambiguous. Here as much as anywhere in Scripture, we can observe the delicate correspondence between the *narrative mode* and the *substantive ambiguity* that is to be articulated. Indeed, it is hard to think how else this substantive ambiguity could have been enunciated, except by way of narrative. The substance requires that mode.[17]

The public façade is broken by the depth of human reality. Thus the king who easily usurps the wife of his general is pressed by prophetic faith until he finally indicts himself and is driven to face his sin (2 Sam. 12:13). That, of course, is not a response expected in a royal chronicle. Thus in chapter 12, the child born to this illicit relationship is killed. And the king grieves. But then, abruptly, the king terminates his grief, as abruptly as the child has been terminated. His action is not expected, and it is not understood by his court. Thus a king who should rejoice over the suppression of a coup, even if a coup by his own son, does not rejoice at all (19:1–8). Instead he grieves. We are given the strange incongruity between a king and a not very good father, who must be cajoled and pistol-whipped by his chief of staff to resume public form. Or in the last episode, the press notices from the palace sound so sure and confident, but we are given to see that they come out of calculating manipulation by the palace junta of an old man who really no longer understands or cares about the issues.

This is not a private, psychological history as though we are to be fascinated by interiority. No, it is a narrative *poised just at the balance point where the pain is most immediate and acute.* The narrator wants us to attend to the deception and the relentless, resilient quality of chagrin and shame and wistfulness that public form never fully nullifies.

Gerhard von Rad, who has provided classic access to this narrative, has related this to the "Solomonic enlightenment."[18] By that he means it lives at a moment of marvelous exaltation of human capacity and human power. For the first time in human history, human motivation and freedom and power are noticed and valued. This narrative serves such a moment of self-assertion. So von Rad writes, "May we not discern in the present historical work the effect of the chill wind of an emancipated spirituality, modernized and freed from cultus?"[19] That is, this narrative is so discerning about human reality that the old postures, structures, and protections are all cut away and the rawness has its powerful say.

Such a notion of "enlightenment" is very different from the one to which we are heir in Western modernity, and von Rad has seen this. "Yet the author is no exponent of 'enlightenment' in the usual sense of the term."[20] That is worth lingering over. For "enlightenment" in the modern world does exactly the opposite of what happens here. The modern enlightenment seeks to reduce life to manageable reasonableness, to cover over and deny and tame the rawness, so that persons are cool and detached. As Karl Barth has seen most clearly,[21] enlightenment intends that human persons become *autonomous*, without reference outside the self. That, I submit, is the dominant presupposition of the culture in which we must now tell these stories, among people like us who imagine ourselves to be reasonable and living in autonomy.

Against such a self-deceiving enlightenment, "the enlightenment" which von Rad has coined for this narrative leads to a massive resistance. Against the modern seduction of tamed rawness, there is here lust and guilt and grief and pathos and vengeance, those elemental tendencies that prevail in spite of all attempts at restraint. Against the modern seductions of autonomy, in understated ways, this narrative does not doubt that David has to do with God. The David who is related to God is a raw, untamed man that none of the forms of the office will cover over. The God with whom David has to do is a God who will not be easily visible, but it is a God who will not let go to permit human persons to choose the shape of their reality.

In our context I suggest that this narrative is distinctively counter-culture, subversive, against our presuppositions.[22] I do not want to modernize it, but the writer is a "master of suspicion" (in Paul Ricoeur's sense), who leaves nothing at face value, but whose narrative sensitivity cuts underneath all the conventions, and invites us to come along in the critique and exposé.[23]

Von Rad has identified the places where the reality of God impinges upon the narrative.[24] We may note how seldom they are, where they are placed, and how they are articulated:

2 Samuel 11:27

Chapters 11—12 of 2 Samuel comprise one narrative unit. This verse comes at the end of chap. 11, the account of Uriah and Bathsheba, just before the narrative moves to chapter 12, the theological reflection which introduces Nathan and the prophetic indictment. This verse, 2 Sam. 11:27, provides the hinge between the exposé of chapter 11 and the reflective indictment of chapter 12. It is laden with heavy simplicity: "The thing David had done was evil in the eyes of Yahweh" (au. trans.). Maybe it was not evil in the eyes of other kings, or in the eyes of the royal establishment. But the eyes of Yahweh see differently and look for different things. The man is not free. The episode is not freestanding. Human conduct is answerable to Yahweh's moral governance. Nobody is immune. And this devastating remark sets in motion chapter 12 with its harsh repudiation. One would not expect anyone to talk that way to a king and live. But one can, if one knows the king is rawly and embarrassingly human.

2 Samuel 12:24-25

The second use noted by von Rad offsets this one. In chap. 12 there has been the first child who dies for the guilt. That moment is over and done with. In 2 Sam. 12:24-25, there is a new son, and this is the one the narrative has its eye on, clear to the end. His name is Solomon, an utterly misnamed child, *shalom*. But the narrative does not blink, even though it knows better. For only the narrative knows what is still to come. There is irony in the name, but for all of that, the narrator stays with the plot. The narrative adds, again laconically, "the Lord loved him" (12:24). That is all. The next verse says, "he called his name Jedidiah [beloved of the Lord], because of the Lord." No explanation. No tracing of the implication. At this point we know nothing, and the narrator seems to have no curiosity, nor to respond to any of ours.

The narrative proceeds quickly in 2 Sam. 12:26 to another fake victory for David. His conquest of Rabbah is perhaps as artificial as his conquest of Bathsheba. Notice how the incongruous words are now lodged in this narrative. The thing was evil (*rā'*). Yahweh loved (*'āhav*). In a family of resilient evil, Yahweh loves. In a history of sordid disobedience, Yahweh makes an abiding commitment. The two do not fit together, but raw, real royal life is like that. We follow the contours of the narrative to find out how that juxtaposition will work. This is not a hopeless account in which evil easily defeats and destroys, because there is love ('āhav). But it is also not a romantic tale in which love conquers all, because love must make its tortured way in the face of stubborn and deep evil. The narrative is a marvelous pursuit of that ambiguity. As such it is an antidote to our modernity which either grows *cynical over evil* or *romantic over love*. On the one hand, we crave romantic self-actualization which thinks evil is a conjuring of super-ego.[25] On the other hand, we are a fearful party in the church, so that when any new creed is written, we want it focused on guilt and punishment and death. But this storyteller insists that in this life with God, they are there together, not sorted out and not to be sorted out, but to be lived with in their lack of resolution.

2 Samuel 17:14

This third reference of von Rad's occurs in the midst of the third episode of the narrative (2 Samuel 15—19). This particular narrative piece consists of a debate between two of Absalom's political advisors on strategies for defeating David. The good advice, which will bring victory, does not persuade. Moreover, the bad advice—a subterfuge planted by David—is heeded even though it brings sure defeat. But readers may be the only ones who see how this odd decision is made. We are the only ones who know. No one in the story except Hushai knows that, and he cannot be sure. We might think that the wrong advice is taken because it is more eloquent or more persuasive or more reasonable, or more daring. But the narrator, in characteristic restraint says only that Yahweh commanded to make ineffectual the good counsel to establish the bad counsel. Two observations on the words.

First, the governing verb is *tsavah*, which we regularly render "command." Here it is often rendered "ordain":

Jerusalem Bible: "determined"

King James Version: "appointed," with a footnote "arranged"

New English Bible: "It was the Lord's purpose"

Clearly the word is a puzzle and is seen to be so by the translators. *Tsavah* as "command" seems too direct and concrete given the narrative context. Who would he command? And so the translators struggle to soften and generalize. But notice that the text itself stays with an old word of sovereignty (*tsavah*). Human operations are never free of that awesome purposing, even if we stutter when we say it.

The other word, "to bring evil" or "to bring evil [counsel]," is the word *rā'*, the word in 11:31, "the thing was evil [*rā'*] in the eyes of Yahweh." I am not sure if the two uses of *rā'* should be closely related, but what is to be observed is that in spite of the tidy juxtaposition of evil/love earlier, here Yahweh is unequivocally on the side of David, perhaps on the side of Solomon in anticipation, against the usurper Absalom. The text is marvelously understated, but the point is not to be missed. The die is already cast. The narrator waits with us to see how it comes to fruition.

1 Kings 2:2–4

Those are the three texts von Rad had noted. I wish to add a fourth from 1 Kings that is of a very different genre. This text clearly does not belong to the light, sophisticated narrative along with the other three.[26] In 1 Kings 2:2–4, we have the charge of old man David to Solomon his beloved son. Most scholars would follow Martin Noth in treating these verses as Deuteronomic.[27] Regardless of its source, in its present location it is a solemn warning growing out of the covenant traditions (vv. 3–4a):

> Keep the charge of the Lord your God, walking in his ways and keeping his statutes, his commandments, his ordinances, and his testimonies, as it is written in the law of Moses . . . that the Lord may establish his word which he spoke concerning me.

It is not a very attractive piece of material. It is openly didactic, in contrast to its narrative context. But it does tie things together. Clearly it looks back to the governing Davidic promise of 2 Samuel 7 (esp. vv. 8–16). But we suggest that it also looks back to 2 Sam. 11:27. The one may be didactic, the other teasing narrative, but they agree on this: Yahweh has not forgotten the difference between good and evil. For all the playfulness of the narrative, the point is consistent and uncompromising. Nathan says, "Why have you despised the word of the Lord, to do what is evil in his sight?" (2 Sam. 12:9). The claim of the law (Torah) is uncompromising. Thus it does not surprise us that even in the final instruction to eliminate the opposition, this word will make its own claim and have its say. For all the delight of enlightenment, there is something brusquely traditional here to which the new men will have to answer. Indeed it is precisely the Torah that presents to us the dilemma and evokes the pain, because the narrator shows the ways in which it is learned that no amount of pain or knowledge diminishes that claim. Human persons are regularly surprised. The surprise is not only external punishment, for David is large enough to avoid that. The surprise is the *interiority* of anguish that does not go away.[28]

The narrator is fascinated by this David who is a man who partakes of all things human. It can be argued that even at the end, as at the beginning, the overriding mark of David is his *self-serving*, even if in the beginning he repents and at the end he urges obedience.

But there are at least two places in which David is portrayed as *a man of stunning faith*. This is more than moral courage of a tragic kind. This is an act of hope which trusts in a live God who can intervene to make a difference. In these two texts (2 Sam. 15:24–29 and 16:12) David is characteristically Israelite and is not to be regarded as Promethean. Both texts show his risk in yielding to the God whom he cannot control and whose will he does not even know for sure. These texts show that David finally yields his life to this other one, and that becomes the ground both of his hope and his strength.[29]

First, in 2 Sam. 15:24–29 David and his priests, Zadok and Abiathar, nicely balanced, are fleeing the holy city in the face of Absalom. They must clearly retreat for the sake of David's safety. As priests are wont to do, they bring the ark with them. The ark is the traditional and sure guarantee of well-being, because it evidences God's sure presence. What king, what human person, would rather not travel in solidarity with the ark?

But David has the capacity to amaze, to do the unexpected. So he says to the priest Zadok (vv. 25–26):

Carry the ark of God back into the city. If I find favor in the eyes of the Lord [these are the same eyes which see evil in 11:27], he will bring me back and let me see both it and his habitation; but if he says, "I have no pleasure in you," behold, here I am, let him do to me what seems good to him. [his eyes, au. trans.]

This is an utter, unreserved yielding. It is not moral courage. It appears not to be calculating. It is genuine abandonment that can only be done by way of narrative. There is no other way to announce it. The statement makes a nice play on the "eyes of Yahweh," for good or for evil. David knows very well that he is being watched and the watcher will decide things.

The second, somewhat parallel, text is 2 Sam. 16:12. David is still in flight. He is taunted along the way by Shimei, who runs alongside shouting abusive things. That, of course, is intolerable, as it is to any governmental officer. And the security officers predictably want to remove the troublemaker. Indeed, they want to kill him. But again, David surprises and says (vv. 11b–12):

> Let him alone, and let him curse; for the Lord has bidden him. It may be ['ûlay] that the Lord will look on my affliction, and that the Lord will repay me with *good* for this cursing of me today. (Italics mine)

Again, David will not take vengeance,[30] even though we might imagine him to be justified in doing-so. Again he casts himself on the Lord, and refuses to exploit. Again, stress is on *the good* which may come from God, that is, to repay good for this cursing. That "good" is in contrast to the evil of 2 Sam. 11:27 and 17:14.

Clearly in this act, David does not conduct himself according to reasons of state. He is much more a man of the tradition. His trust in the power of God to do good even in the face of curse is reminiscent of the Balaam tradition of Numbers 22—24. Now one can argue that David acts here out of character. Perhaps, but I suggest the narrative wants to tell us of this quintessential human being who is still under way, still being "rendered," and not yet settled, now at risk, now being decided, now conforming to oldest modes. The narrator serves as a link between the person of David and the listening community. On the one hand, the narrator attends to the surprising, free concreteness of David. On the other hand, the narrator invites the listening community to watch, to be amazed, and to know itself better, to become aware of alternative ways in the world. David becomes the way in which this narrator announces alternative ways to be in the world.

We are now prepared to consider a text in detail, to consider the painful truth of David. Hopefully this general orientation has prepared us to discern the truth of the narrative more sensitively. As presupposition for that discernment, these conclusions are drawn from our discussion:

1. The narrative is presented in four episodes which are independent and yet which flow in sequence. That sequence is crucial to the claim of the narrative.
2. The anguish at the interface of personal and public life, which both knows "the enlightenment" and protests against "the enlightenment," concerns raw human reality and the pain that is unavoidable.
3. Four statements are offered about Yahweh's relentless rule of a covenantal kind, with an intense dimension, one time explicit (1 Kings 2:2–4), three times inscrutable and suggestive.
4. On two occasions there is evidence that David casts himself fully on that faithful sovereign without regard to himself or appeal to his claims or credentials.

These insights prepare us for a close reading of the text, for a shrewd discernment of David's truth that is not without theological claim, but which draws very close to the man.

BATHSHEBA, URIAH, AND DAVID

We are now prepared to take up the narrative in detail. It is apparent at the outset that David's truth here is peculiarly shrewd and subtle. That shrewdness and subtlety, bearing truth, comes in delicate literary form. Let us look closely at this narrative art, which carries and shapes the claims of the narrator. Our point, which is indeed the point of our entire theme, is that the way of articulation is intimately linked to the substance to be articulated. The way of speaking truth governs much of what we know to be David's truth. We will miss the point unless we observe that the finesse of expression here lets some things be said and known about David that could be neither said nor known without this form of expression.

It is agreed that the narrative of Bathsheba, Uriah, and David (2 Samuel 11—12) is pivotal for the entire narrative. Its presentation and placement are done with extraordinary skill and sensitivity. Our theme poses the question, what is David's truth here?

2 Samuel 11:1 provides an introduction. It makes a public location

with the war that is narrated only in 12:16–31. (See the introduction with the war narrative in 1 Chron. 10:1.) So we have a piece *framed* by public reference points (possibly *inserted*). Alter[31] has seen that this verse creates a wedge for personal life in the midst of public office with the break point put this way: David remained at Jerusalem. Is he honored (cf. 21:17)? Or is he remiss? Does the narrator mean to glorify or accuse? We are not told.

The action, almost the only action in this long account, is contained in 11:2–5. Everything of note happens here and it happens very quickly. The royal action is governed by powerful verbs. David holds all the initiative, because he is king, and no one in the story must forget that:

> It happened, late one afternoon, when David *arose* [*qûm*]
>
> from his couch and was *walking* upon the roof of the king's house, that he *saw* from the roof a woman bathing; and the woman was very beautiful. David *sent* and *inquired* about the woman. . . . So David *sent* messengers, and *took* her; and she came to him and he *lay* with her. . . .
>
> Then she *returned* [*shûv*] to her house.

The entire narrative happens between *qûm* and *shûv*: David "arose" and Bathsheba "returned." End of narrative. King in charge. Just an afternoon's lark. Verse 5, however, lies outside the episode and outside the administration of the king: "the woman conceived." And now, only now, does she speak. This is her first speech. David's only speech has been to inquire about her identity. And even that is not direct discourse. She was, as he presumed, the wife of Uriah the Hittite, which means he could move with little risk. There is no speech in the midst of the seizure, no consent, no resistance. The narrative is carefully created to get to this point. She says only two words, "I'm pregnant" (au. trans.). The world is changed. The king does not govern. An irretrievable act of public implication is now done, and utterly beyond recall. The cover-up must begin.

First Resolution

A first resolution to the problem of 2 Sam. 11:2–5 is offered in 2 Sam. 11:6–11. David is a man of action and decision. No pause. He does not vacillate. Problems are for solving. David knows immediately

what to do. Three times in v. 6 we have the sovereign verb "send."
He had already sent twice in vv. 3–5: "David sent and inquired";
"David sent messengers, and took her." Sending, royal sending, is
what had caused the problem, and now David will resolve it by some
more sending: "So David sent word to Joab, 'Send me Uriah the
Hittite.' And Jacob sent Uriah to David." The three uses of "send" are
matched in verse 7 by three uses of *shalom*, the *shalom* of Joab, the
shalom of the people, the *shalom* of the war. David engages in typical
talk between military men, the man in the field and the man in command.

But military talk will not help, because the problem is not a public
one that will admit of a public resolution. It is easier to win a war than
it is to cover an affront. Public power will not solve personal issues.
David offers Uriah a personal break from the public act of war, tries
to draw him into the personal dilemma. Uriah is given a furlough to
get his wife pregnant (vv. 8–13). David says, "Go down to your house,
and wash your feet." That is enough. The euphemism is understood
by these men from the barracks. The use of the euphemism evidences
that the cover-up is under way. The general is not preoccupied with
personal problems or personal lust, however, and therefore refuses the
king's generosity. Unwittingly he refuses to participate in the king's
rather innocuous resolution. That resolution would have hurt no one,
only a misidentified father. David is not malicious. He simply wants
out, in order to survive.

The exchange between general and commander is governed by the
verb "to go down" (*yarad*):

v. 8, David: "Go down to your house"
v. 9, Narrator: "[Uriah] did not go down to his house"
v. 10, Messengers: "[Messengers] told David 'Uriah did not go down
to his house.'
David said to Uriah, '. . . Why did you not go down to your
house?'"

In the middle of the conversation David understands that this tactic
will not work. Without changing the tone of voice or missing a beat,
David is driven to more desperate action. He will not beg his general,
because kings do not beg generals. He buys him another drink and
sends him off. David's mind is already on the next stratagem, way

ahead of his advisors who must have known something since they reported "He did not go down" (v. 13). Uriah has missed his chance. With a great king you get only one chance. Now that chance is gone. It is time to move to the next measure of jeopardy.

The play on "go down" (*yarad*) shows that David has lost control. In v. 8 he says "Go down," but in v. 13 the narrator concludes shrewdly with a wink, Uriah "did not go down to his house." In that moment David has become a frantic man. His governance is endangered by his guilt, and by his recalcitrant, overly zealous general. David must proceed carefully, however, for the last thing he needs is to arouse the suspicion of Uriah.

Second Resolution

The first resolution did not work, although it was not terribly objectionable. It was only an act of cleverness. A second resolution is offered in 2 Sam. 11:14–25—this one much more ominous. It is an act of desperation. Verse 13 says that "in the evening" Uriah lay on his couch. Verse 14 begins "in the morning." The time has passed quickly (narrative time). We do not need to watch the doomed man sleep. While Uriah slept, David wrote a letter, sometime between evening and morning. We are not told what happened in the night. By sunrise David is a man full of resolve. He knows what to do. The irony is high. The innocent, obedient man sleeps. But the wicked devise evil on their beds, all night long if necessary. (Micah 2:1)

David wrote a letter. He has to issue a formal command. Joab would not undertake such a treachery except on explicit command. He wanted a written order, so that he would not be blamed later. David does not flinch. He knows the fine art of the carefully evasive order. Again the verbs of action prevail: "David wrote, [he] sent, . . . he wrote" (vv. 14–15). He is in charge. He can control Joab. He could not control Uriah. He could not control his passion. He could not control the mystery of pregnancy. But at least Joab will obey, like a good soldier. The command is explicit. It must have been confidential, "for the eyes of the general only." But if it is that confidential, and neither David nor Joab would ever reveal it, how did it get into the narrative? Well, Joab might have leaked it. Better yet, we are dealing with narrative art. This is what should have happened even if it did not. And this is what did happen, because this is the painful truth of the man, the man caught between the torture of an unresolvable moral life and public resolutions which do not go very far.

The unfolding of this second resolution is crafted and subtle. It should not be read simply as a descriptive narrative. Rather, it is a playful, suggestive account in which the narrator means only to hint. By the use of porous words, the reader is invited to "fill out" the suggestions of the narrative. The narrative is remarkably presented, so that even though we know the outcome, there is still a dreadful suspense in the telling.

We may first observe the character of this proposed resolution by seeing the moves of the plot.

vv. 14–15: the *order* is given: "Set Uriah in the forefront of the hardest fighting . . . that he may be struck down, and die"

vv. 16–17: the *execution* of the order with the terse ending: "Uriah the Hittite was slain also"

vv. 18–24: the *report* is made to David. In this narrative, Joab understands exactly what he faces. Is it not remarkable that it takes only two verses to execute! But it takes seven verses to frame a report that is properly ambiguous, with proper duplicity.

v. 25: the *response* of David is given. He is now satisfied. The resolution works. David imagines that the misdeed of vv. 2–5 is now behind him. But he is the only one who thinks so.

It is also possible to trace this crafted statement by following the references to *Uriah*. The narrator has shaped the account so that Uriah and not David is the real actor, even though he does not do anything. This is another example in which the narrator allows for the hiddenness of the historical process to make its own statement:

v. 15: concerning the order, "Set *Uriah* in the forefront"

v. 17: concerning the execution, "*Uriah* the Hittite is dead also"

v. 21: in the report (say to the king), "*Uriah* the Hittite is dead also"

v. 24: in the report, "*Uriah* the Hittite is dead also"

It is worth noting that in the last three uses, vv. 17, 21, 24, the particle "also" (*gam*) is used. Uriah is "also" dead, as an afterthought—"Oh, by the way . . ." The narrator does not want to call too much attention to the Hittite commander, but the narrator also does not want the point to be missed. The most ironic mention of Uriah is in v. 14. The letter, the order which mandated his own death, is carried by the innocent, loyal, noble Uriah. Is there nothing to which David will not stoop for the cover-up? Is there no shame? As recent memory confirms, the cover-up goes way beyond the crime in its shameless, scandalous course.

We can also trace the second resolution through the word "death" (*mûth*). It is precisely this word which dominates the narrative:

v. 15: "that he may be struck down and *die*"

v. 17: "Uriah the Hittite is *dead* also" (au. trans.)

v. 21: "Uriah the Hittite is *dead* also"

v. 24: "Some of the king's servants are *dead*; and your servant Uriah the Hittite is *dead* also"

Five times the note is sounded. The narrative is not intended to transmit information, because the story line is well known and we dare believe the story line was well known in the time of the narrator. Clearly the narrative is not intended to be descriptive, because what is given here goes beyond what is recorded. Partly what we have here is *remembered*. And partly what we have here is *imagined*. The narrative is an imaginative work designed to trace out the truth about David, who can command armies and manage public opinion, but who cannot order his life or govern the gift of life entrusted to him. He is obviously much better at death than at life. And the statement is so subtle, because that fact is a surprise to David, who perhaps thought himself to be "pro-life." The narrative shows David as bearer and agent of death.

David's response to the successful report of Uriah's death is also a way to understand the second resolution. His response is less than noble: "Do not let this thing be evil in your eyes" (v. 25, au. trans.). The wording is important. It may mean do not let it "trouble" you, do not worry, do not feel guilty. But the text shows the king sorting out moral matters. He announces that it is not evil (*rā*'), and the reason it is not evil (*rā*') is that it is the way of war. The death of Uriah is not exceptional and the commander of a mighty army cannot blink over that. It just happens, indiscriminately, now this one and now that one, for war is no respecter of persons. Too bad David's response in chap. 18 to the death of Absalom did not so positively value indiscriminate death in war. There also the messenger brings the news. There also the messenger has reason to think the king will be pleased. But of course he is much more positive about the death of Uriah than the death of Absalom. He is not able to be so coldly philosophical when it is not a Hittite, but his own son.

Even in the dismissal of the death report, however, David knows better, because he had contrived it. Joab knows better, because he had implemented it, and he knew exactly what he was doing. The narrator knows better. We know as much as we can stomach about this David who stayed home. We know about the public use of power for personal ends. We know something about ourselves. We know at least as much as we can stomach—about ourselves. We sense here that David's truth is not unlike our own.

This episode comes to a quick end in vv. 26–27. First the narrator tells how Bathsheba mourned properly and then joined the entourage of David. Notice, she is not named. She had a name, but the narrator will not let it pass his lips. She is only "the wife of Uriah" (v. 26). That is who she is in this narrative. She must never be mistaken for anyone else. Later in the narrative (1 Kings 1 11), she has received another identity, "mother of Solomon." That identity of course changes everything. But even there, "mother of Solomon" is something less than "wife of David." At least in our particular narrative she is not identified with reference either to David or Solomon. She is only "wife of Uriah," and the phrase hangs like an unresolved judgment over the entire scene—over David as well as the woman. No amount of royal cunning or ruthlessness will change her real identity. David is unable to change her real identity as the wife of another man, now slain.

The second surprise at the end of this episode is this: "The thing that David had done displeased the Lord" (v. 27). This is the first mention of Yahweh. The narrative could end here without mention of Yahweh. David imagined the story could be played out in autonomy, without reference to Yahweh. But Yahweh will appear, at the last minute, in order to keep the story going.[32] Whenever Yahweh appears, sooner or later, his appearance marks the decisive moment. Yahweh will not be eliminated from the narrative. Even if he comes very late to the scene of the crime, his coming triggers everything that follows.

Note that the concluding formula, "The thing was evil in the eyes of Yahweh" (v. 27, au. trans.), is a precise and intentional contradiction to David's verdict, "do not let this thing be evil in your eyes" (v. 25, au. trans.). The contrast is complete, even though the parallel is mostly lost in conventional translation. The King James Version comes closest of the readings I have checked, because it preserves the parallel:

> Let not this thing displease thee. (v. 25)
> The thing . . . displeased Yahweh. (v. 27)

But "displease" is weak. The word is "evil" (rā'). What we in fact have is a royal decision that what the Torah community calls evil, David by decree asserts is not evil. It is not evil because the interest of the crown overrides conventional morality. The incongruity is effectively understated, but the narrative means to allude to an overriding moral crisis about good and evil and who gets to decide. Here David practices the very thing the prophets assault:

> Woe to those who call evil good and good evil. (Isa. 5:20)
> Seek good, and not evil. (Amos 5:14)
> Hate evil, and love good. (Amos 5:15)
> You who hate the good and love the evil. (Micah 3:2)
> He has showed you, O man, what is good. (Micah 6:8)

Now the truth begins to emerge: David's truth. We now know about David. What we do not know yet is David's capacity for "crisis management" of this "evil called good" when Yahweh comes on the scene.

Third Resolution

We come now to the third resolution of the crisis created in 2 Sam. 11:2-5. In this narrative report (2 Sam. 12:1-15), we do not have such a playful, subtle presentation. The new factor is Yahweh and Yahweh's prophet. There is still David. There is still the lingering power of Uriah's death. But now there is Yahweh decisively at the center of the narrative. The first resolution was not David's truth, but only a wish for easy escape. The second resolution turned out not to be David's whole truth because Yahweh is not visible. Here we discern David's truth in a new way, a truth that has Yahweh at its center. This episode has a kind of moral earnestness that diminishes the artful playfulness we have seen in the two preceding efforts. This narrative is nicely framed:

> The Lord sent Nathan to David. (v. 1)
> Nathan went to his house. (v. 15)

At the outset, it is important that Yahweh now is the one who sends, not David. The momentum has shifted. David is no longer an active agent, but only a recipient of the word from Yahweh.

In 2 Sam. 12:1–5, we have a parable and David's response. The parable is remarkable in itself. Good parables score their point in a variety of contexts, but what interests us more is that a parable is the chosen mode of communication. Indeed, it must be.[33] One cannot address royal power directly, especially royal power so deeply in guilt. It is permissible to talk about speaking truth to power, but if truth is to have a chance with power, it must be done with some subtlety.[34]

In 12:6–12 we are given a classic lawsuit speech, which does not allow great space for playfulness. The use of such a traditional form immediately after the parable is an experience of imaginative wrenching. Just when the parable suggests a kind of open-endedness, the lawsuit drives home the point with overriding clarity. The indictment begins in a way faithful to the structure of covenantal speech, with a review of gracious deeds. The recital is reminiscent of that in 2 Sam. 7:8–10. But the recital does not cancel out the beginning point which rings in the ears of David: "You are the man" (v. 7). Now on the lips of the prophet is a word which matches the word of Bathsheba for terseness and poignancy: "I am pregnant" (au. trans.). David gets the awful truth from earth and from heaven. The woman says, "I am pregnant." The prophet says, "You are the man."

In 12:9 we are offered a heavily loaded indictment which is unarguable. David does not argue. The dreaded word is used and it cannot be disputed. You have done what is evil in the eyes of Yahweh. It is the same phrase as in 11:27. Now it is irrelevant that it looked differently to your eyes and to the eyes of Yahweh. The king and his hatchet men are not the arbitrators of what is good and evil. It is evil, and there is no royal privilege or immunity. The accusation is threefold:

> You have smitten Uriah.
> You have taken his wife.
> You have killed him.

The verb "to kill" is a harsher word. Our verb has been "to die" (*mûth*). Now it is "to kill" (*harag*). The rhetoric of chapter 11 indicated "Uriah is dead." Now Nathan gets it right. "You have killed" (Revised Standard Version, "slain"). It is action. Uriah did not die from passivity but from an act of enormous guilt. Passive verbs are wonderful. They let the action be described, but without suggesting there is an agent who must answer. Kings love to speak with passive verbs: "At 1100 hours the bomb was dropped." It is the power of narrative to locate the agent, and then to call the agent to give answer.

The charges against David are, of course, unanswerable, and are quickly put. Nathan's sentencing of David is more complicated (12:10–11; cf. 16:22):

> The sword shall never depart from your house. . . . I will raise up evil against you out of your own house; and I will take your wives before your eyes, and give them to your neighbor.

There is that word "evil" (rā') again. It keeps turning up. Patrick Miller has observed that this verdict on the part of Nathan is a model for how the Bible thinks about such issues:

> This general theological statement, which is spelled out in both cases as to the particulars of David's rā' and of Yahweh's rā'(ah), is a kind of paradigm of the correspondence motif in its most general expression. Rā' leads to rā'. The rā' (evil) of the sin leads to the rā' (punishment) of the judgment. A model is thus produced to express the correspondence device in nuce: rā' (human)—rā' (divine). This general model undergirds the form of the correspondence in several other examples and in some sense may be presumed to be the theological basis of the correspondence between sin and judgment in general.[35]

There is a threat here to royal power. There is also utter humiliation. The lawsuit surprises David—and us. He had imagined he could out-flank the cost of evil, but the narrator knows that he cannot.

There is still one more surprise. David repents. "I have sinned against the Lord" (12:13). Who would have thought him capable of that? Repentance after lawsuit is here as unexpected as lawsuit was after David's second resolution. David's response permits the following settlement: David will not die (v. 13) and the child that is born to David will surely die (v. 14). Death does not strike the man. But death hovers. And in the long run, perhaps hovering death is worse than accomplished death.

The most interesting structural question may be the relation of 2 ₁

Samuel 11 to 2 Samuel 12. Chapter 12 is didactic when contrasted with chapter 11. Does chap. 12 stifle and cancel 11? Or is chap. 11 only a staging area for 12? It is a literary question, but also a theological question, because it asks about *playful freedom* and *dreadful account-ability*. In the mix of these two perspectives is the painful truth of this man, and perhaps every human person. Truth does not come clear unless both chapters are taken together. The narrator did not want and was not able to choose between them. David's painful truth lives somewhere between these alternative resolutions. The decisive voice of the third resolution does not nullify the power of the first two resolutions in showing us some of the truth about David and about us.

Soon after the assassination of John F. Kennedy, Patrick Moynihan, then a part of the administration, had the right words when asked about resuming life after that event. He said, "We shall laugh again, but we shall never be young again." That is how it is with David and with all who enter this narrative and find their truth here. David and his company will laugh again, but they will never be young again.

3

THE SURE TRUTH
OF THE STATE

(2 SAMUEL 5:6—8:18)

W<small>E HAVE CONSIDERED</small> the two extended narratives about David, "The Rise of David" (chap. 1) and "The Succession Narrative" (chap. 2). We have tried to show that they have different orientations, proceed in different ways, and perform different social functions—the first as an uncritical celebration of "the chieftain" on the make; the second as a critical reflection on "the man" who is in disarray. Now we want to characterize a third way of narrative truth which I have termed "The Sure Truth of the State."

PRELIMINARIES

Before turning to the text, I want to begin with two preliminary critical comments. First, the text I have designated "The Sure Truth of the State," refers to 2 Samuel 5—8, and especially chaps. 7 and 8. Although this literature is of crucial importance, our critical judgments are obscure and open to revision. Most scholars are inclined to end the tribal tale somewhere in chap. 5: A. F. Campbell continues through 5:12, and begins the Succession Narrative with chap. 9.[1] David M. Gunn would split it differently and include chaps. 2—4 in the Succession Narrative.[2] Even if one follows Gunn and pushes the Succession Narrative earlier, this would still not include chaps. 5—8 which he brackets out. Only by following Aage Carlson[3] or Robert Alter[4] would these be included, and as noted, neither Carlson nor Alter has made a case we can follow. Carlson has not won any significant scholarly support, nor has Alter made the case in any substantive way. While the articulations vary, scholars generally recognize that chaps. 5—8, or at least 6—8, are not readily linked to either of the major narratives we have thus far studied.

Second, notice that I have used the phrase, "the truth of the state," which I mean to contrast with our earlier discussions of "the truth of the tribe." I appeal to the judgment that *tribe* and *state* are the key social models in the ancient world and in the Old Testament, and in this I follow especially the categories of Norman K. Gottwald.[5] The "tribe" is a social model of egalitarianism and the "state" (not the city) is a completely shifted social organization in which there is a monopoly of the means of production and the concentration of social power in the hands of a ruling elite.

That sociological difference (asserted as a model and not argued here empirically) refers to political and economic power. But with it, I argue, there is also a shift in epistemology, so that what is true is what is useful to the monopoly. Truth thus becomes "interested" in a much more intentional, deliberate, and controlling way. Truth now becomes enmeshed in a scarcity system. That is, scarcity is produced and administered by monopoly, so that some have too much at the expense of others.[6] When goods are organized into a scarcity system, then epistemological matters must also be managed to support and sustain the distribution. State secrets must be transmitted and protected. Censorship becomes essential. The news must be managed. Now every society has some of this, even if it is only gossip at the village well, which is a way to manage the news. But it is clear enough that economic and political monopoly evoke a parallel monopoly of knowledge. In modern terms, the management of scarcity and the control of information are related to the quantity of political prisoners. And when one thinks this way, one is not too far removed from the tone of the administration of Solomon.

I propose that in these chapters, especially 2 Samuel 7—8, we have reflected in reportage on David a shift in such a sociological, epistemological direction. We need not say that this has to do with the historical David, or that in his historical moment, the transition is made. Frank M. Cross[7] and many others believe that the decisive break is not between Saul and David, but between David and Solomon. It is Solomon, not David, who completely reshapes Israel's life and therefore Israel's epistemology. Thus it is entirely plausible to argue that these chapters are a Solomonic rather than Davidic construct. Indeed that is much more likely. Such an identification of the provenance of this literature permits the Solomonic enterprise to use David as a way of presenting this new truth

Such a likelihood is important for our understanding of this narrative act, because the implication of such a sociological shift is that there is a parallel intellectual shift and with it a shift in narrative intent as well. This has everything to do with Scripture interpretation. What we have in these chapters is not a literary unit—at least not in the sense of the Succession Narrative—but a collection of different materials that are best understood in relation to the sociological changes which evoke them, and which these chapters helped to legitimate and authorize.

INFLUENCES ON OUR APPROACH

Two discussions have been decisive for shaping the categories through which I have approached this literature.

The first of these is *The King David Report* by Stefan Heym.[8] Heym is an East German literary figure. In this novel he constructs a notion of how the David materials came to be written as they were. He conjures that at the initiative of King Solomon, there was a committee charged to produce a literary glorification of David, in order to enhance the legitimacy of Solomon which needed all the help it could get. That is, its work is the generation of literature that serves a quite specific political end. It is clear that Heym understands the material to be ideological, that is, truth in the service of the regime.

On this committee are Beniah, the chairman of the joint chiefs of staff, and Zadok, Solomon's high priest. Note that they are the survivors in the bureaucratic jungle after the purge of Abiathar, the alternative priest, and Joab, the older military man (1 Kings 1:38; 2:26–35). These are the new young ones whose success is much too recent. The purpose of the committee is to produce ideological literature in the service of Solomon, but each of these committee members also has his own political well-being to consider along with that of the king. The mockery is that they must write ideology, but they must be generative and imaginative about it, almost a contradiction in terms.

As Heym imagines it, this committee hires a skilled but frightened scribe to write things down, because none of the principal men has such a skill. This nobody of a scribe is cast in a hopeless role, because he dares not displease any member of the committee or his life will be endangered. Yet obviously he cannot please them all, because they have very different truths they want to express, or at least they have very different versions of Solomonic truth they want to serve.

The point of Heym's work, and the reason I cite it, is that the text as we have it has been carefully handled and shaped and managed to serve political interests. One can tell that the text has such usage, according to Heym, for it is to be called:

The One and Only True and Authoritative, Historically Correct and Officially Approved Report on the Amazing Rise, God-Fearing Life, Heroic Deeds, and Wonderful Achievements of David the Son of Jesse, King of Judah for Seven Years and of both Judah and Israel for Thirty-three, Chosen of God, and Father of King Solomon.

Heym adds, "For short called The King David Report."[9] It is important to note that Heym treats the whole of the David account under this single rubric, without appealing to the distinction conventionally made in critical scholarship. I appeal to his work at this point, however, because I believe these chapters we are studying are especially linked to his claim. Of course, I do not suggest, and certainly Heym does not suggest, that the tribal narrative is disinterested. But it is not, I believe, so calculatingly shaped as is this material.

It is clear to you, I hope, that Heym is not in fact writing about the Davidic material. His appeal to the Davidic material is heuristic, because his intention is to comment on the way in which his own totalitarian regime manipulates truth for the sake of the regime. It should come as no surprise to know that Heym is frequently in trouble with the regime. He has observed how memory is daily turned into propaganda, and he has the temerity to suggest that the same thing is happening in the Bible.

I find Heym suggestive at two levels. First, and mainly, I believe Heym's way of envisioning the origin of this literature is quite plausible. The problem is that such a propagandistic act is the bearer of our best theological truth. The second level is that this is exactly how the

Bible is used among us, in the church and in civil religion generally; that is, it is understood as a piece of propaganda to legitimate our special social interests. My critical suggestion is that we need to help people see that such propaganda is the vehicle used by the Bible to articulate our best faith, and that we use these texts largely for purposes of propaganda. A recent review of the life of Katherine Anne Porter said that her life story was "a set of carefully selected pieces of fiction." It is so of David and those who follow in his train.

The second discussion that has informed me is *The Saga Mind* by M. I. Steblin-Kamenskij.[10] This book argues that there are two kinds of truth,[11] the one is reflected in the social awareness and modes of knowledge served by the saga, which Steblin-Kamenskij calls "syncretic" truth. That is, it is a way of characterizing reality that does not split the artistic from the historical. This truth is taken as an anonymous given, not criticized as invention, not identified by author, but simply taken as the way in which reality is known, albeit uncritically and with reasonable disinterest. One may suggest that something like this is what Walter Ong has in mind for an oral society.[12]

But as power becomes concentrated in the hands of bishops or kings, we begin to get the emergence of a new truth, which is intentional and self-conscious, in which truth is what is advantageous to the church, or to whatever the center of power may be called. This second kind of truth Steblin-Kamenskij calls "state truth," in which there are now known authors and artistic factors serving other ends, in which the interest of institutions and individuals begins to be expressed quite explicitly.[13] I am not sure what overlap there may be between the polemic of Heym and the critical analysis of Steblin-Kamenskij, but I think they point very much in the same direction. As the social organization shifts, as there is a monopoly of power and wealth, so there is a shift in the modes of disclosure, and what had been *disclosure* becomes a mode of *mystification*. A different way with the narrative is required to carry that truth.

UNAMBIGUOUS TRUTH

I have called this "the sure truth of the state." The adjective is important. This literary statement is very different from "the painful truth" of the Succession Narrative. In 2 Samuel 5—8 there is no pain, no anguish or ambiguity, no permission to see behind things. In 2 Sam. 19:5–7 Joab rebukes David for not presenting a good public face. He warns David that if his personal pain is allowed to erode a good public presence, the whole fragile "house of authority" will quickly collapse. In contrast to such pain-filled candor, this narrative is sure and unambiguous. This is nothing other than the unfootnoted public fact.

In a similar way, this sure truth is unlike the trustful truth of the tribe. The tribe really believed its narrative, and it took it uncritically. Such a text invites a childlike retelling, and that is what we are inclined to do with some of the lovely and teasing stories of the tribe. The material of 2 Samuel 5—8, I propose, is not trustful with any naiveté. It is sure and self-confident. Indeed this literature is cynical enough to know that the reports must be written to justify the state's case for execution of the war.[14] If some of the details of facticity must be disregarded or slanted or covered over, this truth must have priority. In the move from tribe to state, we are moving into ideology, into a justification of present forms of power and social organization and into propaganda, in which truth is what is advantageous.[15] Note, I do not argue that this is dishonest or lightly perverted. I argue rather that the shift of perception caused by a monopoly of wealth and power invites such distortion, which then becomes systematic distortion. In the telling and retelling of these narratives, the distortion must be transmitted, for the distortion is systematic and pervasive. I do not believe there is a predistorted text of these things. That is, there never was a "Nathan oracle" which was not ideologically intentional. Moreover, I shall say that this "sure truth," distorted as it is, is foundationally the vehicle for important faith resources. Perhaps the test of the quality of narrative here and the truth it bears is evidenced in that these are not the stories we tell our young. There is something about them that does not invite imagination or freedom or delight. I suggest that is because the truth now is too earnest, with too much at stake for too few.

ROYAL THEOLOGY

The texts that will primarily concern us are 2 Samuel 7—8. Chapters 5 and 6 could be used, but they are more of a mixed lot. It is agreed that 2 Samuel 7 is the decisive text for understanding David. It is placed in the tradition just at the pivot point between "the Rise of David" and "the Succession Narrative," or in Carlson's scheme, just at the turn from blessing to curse.

2 Samuel 7:1–7[16]

These verses are preliminary to the main point. In 7:1–3, David has direct and immediate access to the prophet, or equally telling, the prophet has immediate access to the king. It will not be so with Solomon. David is portrayed as the utterly faithful king, for what faithful kings do is build temples. David now proposes to do what a good king should do. He is finally ensconced and is no longer a chieftain, for chieftains do not build temples. But kings do, and must, and should. The narrative begins in an uncritical way. David gets immediate approval to do what kings do to show their piety. One wonders if there is irony here, for the text nicely contrasts the luxuriant life of the king with the shabby treatment of God (cf. Jer. 22:13–16). What strikes one most about this text, however, is the abruptness of the theme. David has been a chieftain all this time, worrying about war and sex and popularity. Now all of a sudden, he wants to act like a king. Suddenly there is a move into a new role, with all the rights and privileges pertaining thereto. No more tribal conflict. No more raids like a guerrilla leader. And if we may believe it, here there is no lust for the wife of another man. Now here is a man of competence, thoughtfulness, studied and measured. He sounds like the completely public man who has no private life. It is like wanting to be "presidential" all at once.

In 2 Sam. 7:4–7 we are put on notice that this conventional state truth of the king as pious temple builder is under heavy review. Nathan's dream of vv. 4–7 challenges the very approval Nathan has just given in v. 3. We do not know what to make of this. It is rather a rebuke for such bland royal thinking. Too much had been taken for granted in the happy link between king and God. Now it is time for high theology, for Yahweh here disassociates himself from conventional royal religion. Maybe all the kings build temples, and all the gods like temples, but not this God and therefore not this king. David is not permitted to act like people in his role act.

One might imagine at this point that we have a break with state truth for the sake of the old memories. We have here a marvelously free God who does not yearn for a temple in ways characteristic of Canaanite deities. The assertion that the God of David has not had a house (7:6) to dwell in is an important assertion, most in keeping with the old tribal truth. But as we read on, we discover that state truth is not broken. It is only intensified and pushed to make an even more radical claim for the crown. Indeed, one might think that vv. 4–7 after vv. 1–3 are a strategy to heighten the claim.

2 Samuel 7:8–17

Here we meet the highest "royal theology" in Israel. (There is no doubt that this passage has had redactional work done on it and that some parts are later than other parts. The specific distinctions are very difficult to make, but none of that detracts from its main claims.)

In 2 Sam. 7:8–12 we have a historical review presented together with the key dynastic promise. The historical review in vv. 8–9 shows how the history of David is a kind of reenactment of the whole history of Israel. This man is indeed the bearer of all of Israel's memory. It all comes to fulfillment here. One can see the formation of state truth, in which everything is consolidated around this very concrete reference.

In 2 Sam. 7:10–12 the dynastic promise is nicely asserted in two parts. In vv. 10–11 this is the promise of a secure place, perhaps land, perhaps city. The words are "place" (v. 10), "rest" (v. 11), and "house" (v. 11). The words are crafted in a richly ambiguous way with special attention to the word "house." This wordplay is famous but not therefore unimportant. In vv. 2–7, the word "house" refers to the temple which David would build, which Yahweh neither wants, needs, nor permits. This state truth breaks with convention. But in v. 12 "house" refers to dynasty, which Yahweh would build for David and which David wants even more than he needs. It seems so obvious. The narrative seems to flow so easily to this conclusion that we must not miss the way in which a new truth has emerged. We are back to the claims of the state more than we were with the previous use of "house" as temple. In the old tribal memory (back to Gideon in Judges 8:22), in the old tribal warning of Samuel (1 Sam. 8:10–17), and in some subtle way in the old tribal legislation (Deut. 17:14–20), there was a consensus that Israel must have no king but Yahweh, and that kingship is inimical to Israel's way in the world.[17] And now, in one grand literary gesture, properly framed for purposes of authority, in one dream dreamed by a royal prophet while he slept in the royal palace, the old truth is overcome by this new truth. The old truth against kingship in deference to the kingship of Yahweh is nullified. It is done in the name of continuity, as it must always be, with the God who lives in a tent. The whole of these verses contains a striking incongruity of a *dynasty* now authorized and guaranteed by a God who will live in a *tent*. But large portions of undigested truth are easily swallowed in the interest of propaganda. Regimes tend not to scruple over such matters that other people perceive as problematic. It is asserted only once, and the argument moves on with the new claim now become the new baseline, never reexamined, but the premise for all that follows. That is how truth functions when it has strong allies.

It takes imagination, shrewdness, and boldness to articulate a new truth that violates the old trustful truth and to present it as more of the sense of shamelessness (cf. Jer. 8:12). One never knows about such a move, whether it is sheer cynicism or if the devotees of the new possibilities are so taken with them that they themselves believe. Thus, for example, in the new presidential "truth of executive privilege,"[18] one has the impression that the blind advocates of presidents are so completely consumed with the office that what appears to be shamelessness is in fact a kind of smittenness that ought not to happen with grown persons. But one never knows. And one does not know in this case about David and Nathan.

We should not easily move past the oddity that 2 Sam. 7:13 authorizes the building of a temple. This is the very temple (with the use of the word "house" again) that has just been rejected as not needed and not wanted and not permitted in vv. 4–7. It is true that almost all critical scholars agree that v. 13 is even later than other editorial activity in this chapter. It is to be taken as a tendentious statement read back from Solomon, likely in relation to 1 Kings 8. But that critical judgment does not lessen the scandal and the shamelessness of the move made in state truth, even if it is a somewhat later move. It is still a move of state truth. The reality is that no dynasty here envisioned can long endure without a temple of some kind to embody and enact transcendent legitimacy, as even the Kremlin leaders have understood with reference to the tomb of Lenin. The critical decision about v. 13 should not blind us to the social necessity of this verse and its anticipation of what is to come. If it did not come in the original version of the text, it had to come—sooner or later![19]

The point is that state truth has the nervy capacity to articulate the very antithesis of old truth in the name of that same old truth. That is what is happening here. Not only the derivative statement on temple in 7:13, but the basic statement of dynasty is problematic. One can understand all of this on pragmatic, political grounds (as Baruch Halpern has shown so well), but we are here considering the theological problematic. Handling this narrative requires sensitivity to the incongruity between historical necessity and theological problematic. The dynasty must have all of this, but one would not expect it to be granted by this God.

In order to grasp the weightiness of the incongruity, I cite this contemporary analogy. Richard Nixon made a career out of communism. He was a key voice in the China lobby in California that supported Taiwan. It is one of the truly great acts of state truth that it was precisely Nixon who found the language, the nerve, and the rationale to make a place for China as an ally. Reasons of state required it. And one can imagine that politically only Nixon (and not a liberal Democrat) could have brought it off. What is most remarkable is that state truth makes new political realities possible.

Finally, 2 Sam. 7:14–16 offers the most extraordinary language to legitimate the fresh departure in theology and politics. The lead sentence of v. 14 establishes a relation of God and king as father and son. The royal claim now has preempted Israel's son status (cf. Exod. 4:22; Hosea 11:1), so that the son is now king and not Israel.[20] The community is now reduced to the king. The claims of the tribal confederation are now transferred to the state. The state now embodies and monopolizes the old images, metaphors, power, and legitimacy that goes with the claim of the federation.

In 7:14–15 we are treated to this most decisive, surprising statement: "When there is sin, God will punish" (au. trans.). Of course that had to be said in a covenantal context. Nobody, not even the king, is free of covenantal requirements and covenantal punishments. But then in

v. 15: "But my abiding loyalty (hesed) I will never remove as I removed it from Saul" (au. trans.). The overriding "if" of covenant faith has been abolished (cf. Exod. 19:5).[21] Now this linkage is at bottom unconditional. There is, so it is claimed, no circumstance that will cause Yahweh to pull away from David and David's family.

The concluding formula of 7:16 contains two phrases of special note. First, the dynasty is made "sure" (ne'emān), utterly reliable (cf. 1 Sam. 25:28). The whole enterprise will be established 'ad-'ôlam, for all the thinkable future—"forever." It is clear now why the tradition has used the adjective "sure" to characterize this promise. It is unambiguous, without any doubt, not conditional. There is no playfulness about it as the other narratives might have entertained. It is now flat, one-dimensional language in which the single interest is unchallengeable certitude. We can scarcely guess at the discussion or the exploration that went on before this press release was issued, whether we think it was issued from God's throne in the divine council or from the star council of the palace. We do not know what kind of theological discomfort was experienced among those who formulated this new thing. They must have experienced exhilaration, but also awareness that they had now taken a fundamental departure from all traditional Israelite notions, for it was a daring move out of the precarious historical process to find religious certitude more guaranteed than anything Israel had ever previously envisioned.

But if we do not know about the *theological method* by which this was concluded, we can surmise the *political function* of the statement, whether we think it is crass and calculating, or whether it is the innocent word of zealous devotees. Either way, Israel's religious possibilities are now all contained precisely here and nowhere else. All the hopes and fears of Israel are met in David, and nowhere else! Anyone who wants to participate in this ongoing history of liberation must now come to terms with this particular regime. David's ideologues have now preempted Israel's memories and faith.

2 Samuel 7:18–29

The oracle must have an answer. When God speaks that way, some response must be given. Israel is entitled to know how David received and responded to this staggering dream oracle, so we are offered an official version of what David said upon hearing the news. Again it is impossible to know how much of this is genuine, passionate faith and how much of it is more contrived speech by the ideologues in the palace. We can at least note that the prayer of response is highly stylized, that there is little here of the passionate man we have seen in other parts of the literature. We may hazard the judgment that this response is as calculating as the originary oracle appears to be.

Kings who have just had the world irreversibly handed over to them tend to pray in reliable, disciplined, calculating ways. In the practice of state truth one does not expect passionate prayer anymore than one expects self-disclosure on the part of a leader of a military junta. One does not know if that is only because of restraint and discipline or whether, after a while, such a public figure becomes incapable of any but the most formal, rationalized gestures. Perhaps it is the only way left for him to pray.

In any case, David answers Yahweh in kind. It may be useful to suggest that even this prayer is state truth. By that I do not mean it is deliberately ideological, though it may be. Rather I mean it is predictably reflective of that social context and those social interests. People with empires to maintain undoubtedly pray differently, at least in public, probably also in private.

In 2 Sam. 7:18–21 there is a statement of formal *deference*. Three times (vv. 19, 20, 21), David refers to himself as "servant," as servant of Yahweh even if none other. To match that, God is addressed four times in these verses as "Lord God" (*Adonai Yahweh*). This form of address dominates the entire prayer. The formula perhaps had special dynastic implication, implying a special linkage between this God (who is incomparable, v. 18), and this dynasty, which by inference is equally incomparable.[22] The third factor to observe is that the use of the word "small" (*qaton*; cf. 1 Sam. 16:11), also used in the parallel prayer of Solomon (1 Kings 3:7), is also a deferential statement crediting all to God. The prayer in both cases is shaped so that one cannot tell if it is serious faith or simply court talk. I suggest that all such talk about servanthood and smallness needs to be treated carefully, if not suspiciously, because nothing in fact is conceded about political power. Everything is retained, in spite of the rhetoric.

In 2 Sam. 7:22–24 we have a *doxology* which further serves to enhance Yahweh, and derivatively to enhance the people Israel and their king. Again the address is to the Lord God. Again the incomparability of Yahweh is asserted, twice in v. 22. In v. 23 the incomparability of Israel is asserted as the entire saving history is mobilized, as we remember that in vv. 10–12 that whole history was claimed for David and his dynasty. The doxology moves then to assert that Israel is forever and Yahweh's commitment to Israel is also forever. We had better approach any such doxology suspiciously.

The word "forever" is a clue word, because when it occurs we are likely dealing with state truth.[23] That point would perhaps not be noticeable if Yahweh were forever. But it is the people Israel that is said to be "forever." By such a rhetorical move, the main jeopardy from the dreaded God has been removed for the dynasty. Yahweh has now been claimed as a friendly and reliable patron for the regime.

When doxology is used in the context of state truth, it has a political function. Ostensibly it enhances God, but when used as it is used here, it has a political function. Praise of God is by necessary implication praise of and legitimization of the regime. So the "foreverness" is processed as a dynastic claim. The deference of vv. 18–21 has been put to quite unexpected use in the doxology of vv. 22–24. What has appeared to be a way of distancing the holy God from this poor servant has turned out to be a way of drawing uncritically close, nearly to the point of identification.[24] It is then no wonder that free, impressionistic narrative has been superseded by a tight line of imperial reasoning that does not find it amusing when people criticize or think in alternative modes. When the distance is overcome between Yahweh and Israel, then there is no room left for ambiguity or playfulness or exploration. And indeed the rhetoric wishes precisely to eliminate all such room, for the banishment of playful room makes things secure. State truth tends not to be marked by a sense of humor. The moves of *deference* and *doxology*, I submit, show the linkage between political function of the language and the mode of expression. Certitude for the regime requires a rather flat statement of the claim.[25] The language must be as one-dimensional as the purpose.

After the *deference* of 2 Sam. 7:18–21 and the *doxology* of 7:22–24, we have the *demand* of 7:25–29. This is a remarkable prayer, but it is almost so stylized that we do not notice. Again there is the repeated use of the formula, "Lord God." But there are other features that suggest this is an articulation of state truth.

This part begins "And now." The word *we 'attah* ("and now") is used three times (vv. 25, 28, 29). It is a term used to move abruptly from past recall to present reality.[26] But it is a term usually used by the strong party to impose something on the lesser party. In the oracle, Yahweh has used the term in v. 8 to change the subject abruptly from temple to dynasty. It could therefore be argued that David uses the term in a way that corresponds to Yahweh's use in v. 8. But David uses it three times. I suggest that, theoretically, David has gone very far in inverting the relationship and taking the initiative for the relation with God. That is exactly what we expect from state truth, with reference to God. Its program is to make God a responsive patron.

In 7:26 we have a shrewd piece of dynastic self-service. It is promised that Yahweh's name will be magnified: "The Lord of hosts is God over Israel, and the house of thy servant David will be established before thee." David here has taken a very old exalted name, "Lord of the troops," but he has now linked it to the dynastic claim. He has fixed it so that Yahweh cannot be magnified unless David is magnified as well. Thus David is linked to Yahweh. And along the way, Israel is identified with David. David here anticipates the enormous claims made by General Charles DeGaulle about his connection with France—"I am France."

Verse 27 acknowledges that David's prayer is one of nerve and effrontery. David explains how he received the "heart" to pray this way (which in the Revised Standard Version is rendered "courage"). David's courage is indeed courage, almost to the point of shamelessness.

We may note one other most interesting juxtaposition. Six times in these verses David refers to himself as "servant," a proper way of deference. Four times in these verses the term "forever" is used. We therefore see that this is a careful and calculating theology. On the one hand, it properly recognizes that David has no claim to make, because he is so little and unworthy. But he has heart to make the claim anyway, because Yahweh has made a commitment, and the real intent of David's prayer is to hold Yahweh firmly and uncompromisingly to his commitment. Yahweh did not need to make such a promise, but since that promise has been made, there is no way David will permit Yahweh to renege or escape it.

The prayer is thus the perfect counterpart to the oracle. The oracle is Yahweh's incredible commitment to a particular historical institution. The prayer is the verification of that commitment. The most intentional sign of direct linkage is that the dynastic oracle of 7:11 is repeated in the prayer by David in 7:27. You said it. Now do it. Only the verb is different. In the oracle it is "make" (*āsah*) and in the reprise it is "build" (*banah*). The second verb maintains the ambiguity of dynasty/temple, but the context refers it precisely to dynasty and not to temple.

EMPIRE BUILDING

After the foundational statement of chap. 7, the claims of chap. 8 will not surprise us greatly.[27] They may be seen as statements of empire building, externally and internally.

2 Samuel 8:1–14

This is a summary of David's conquests and subjugation of all neighboring territories. What may most interest us is how uninteresting it all is. The imperial record is not much interested in attractive communication or finesse.

First, one needs to observe the four verbs that tell the story:

The dominant verb is "to smite" (*bakah*), which is weakly rendered in the Revised Standard Version, "defeat," used in v. 1 of the Philistines, in v. 2 of Moab, in v. 3 of Hadadezer, and in v. 10 of Toi. The rendering "defeat" purges the word a bit of its savage and concrete connotation which suggests that David did not fool around. Most interesting is its use in v. 10, where a peace mission is sent, but David is not much for negotiations. He continues to be a man of very peculiar "shalom."

The second verb is "to take" (*laqah*) in vv. 7 and 8, and seconded by *lahad* in v. 4. It is a verb used, among other things, for the seizure of war booty, especially the confiscation of temple objects for reassignment to the shrine of Yahweh. The verb expresses David's rapacious way that is all intertwined with his religion. It is, incidentally, the verb used in 11:4 for the "taking" of Bathsheba.

The third verb is surprising. *Qôdesh* is used twice in v. 11, rendered in the Revised Standard Version as "dedicate"; it means to make holy or submit to the holy claims of Yahweh. It is an odd statement in a passage on conquest. If this were tribal, then one could argue that David practiced the old tribal act of devotion which Saul in 1 Samuel 15 foolishly violated. But I think not. The term *herem* ("fully devoted by destruction") is not used and such an act would be incongruous with David's way here. *Qôdesh* reflects another usage here. We have a self-serving monarchy that has established itself as a zone of sanctity or sacredness, making the dynasty itself transcendent and therefore beyond criticism. In contrast to *herem* used by the tribe, I suggest *qôdesh* here bespeaks a hierarchal understanding of reality, precisely the kind needed for state truth.[28]

The fourth verb in v. 11 in *kabash*, rendered in the Revised Standard Version as "subdued." The term is used in Gen. 1:28 for "subdue the earth," suggesting that David is on his way to making claims as the Adamic man. It can be plausibly argued that the term is a good traditional tribal word for conquest (cf. Josh. 18:1; Num. 32:22, 29). But I suggest that with *kabash* as with *qôdesh*, we have hints that David is on the way to a transformed vocabulary, reflective of the transformed social and political situation.

The other thing to observe in this listing of triumphs is the double use of the formula, "the Lord gave victory to David wherever he went" (8:6, 14). Heym[29] has his scribe characterize this as the concluding general comment of the bureacratic summary. The word "victory" renders *yāša'*, "liberation." But the meaning in context is clear. This is exactly the claim one would expect after the commitments of Yahweh in 2 Samuel 7. Indeed, given the remarkable rise of David, surely no other conclusion could be drawn. But note carefully the contrasting statement of v. 13, "David won a name for himself." In this moment of self-congratulation which the regime could scarcely resist, all the theological niceties and acts of deference are forgotten. David, not Yahweh, is credited. The promise of chap. 7 is for the moment shelved and the new reality in world history is credited simply to its human perpetrator. That also smacks of state truth, for the old tribal chieftains would have been incapable of such a moment of self-congratulations. (This way of self-naming is in contrast to 1 Kings 1:47, where Yahweh is credited with having given the name. Here David does it himself.)

2 Samuel 8:15–18

The last paragraph of 2 Samuel 8 (8:15–18) appears to be something of an addendum for the sake of completeness. It places in tension three very different motifs, which suggest that this perception of reality has no great patience with all of the distinctions others might have drawn. The regime has no time for such nuanced articulation.

First, in 8:15 David "reigns" (*malak*). There is now no ambiguity. There is no concern to tone it down, to claim that David is regent for Yahweh or anything like that. There is no avoidance of the term *malak* by a circumlocution like *nagîd* or *nāsi'*. This narrative is unembarrassed about who is in charge.

The second element, the surprise of v. 15, is that David does "justice and righteousness" (*mišpaṭ* and *ṣedeqah*). It is difficult to know what to make of this statement. It could be a cliché that just needs to be repeated, no matter what. It could be that kings doing "justice and righteousness" is the main claim of the dynasty, the identifying slogan, a public commitment of state truth, as Republicans must recite the claims of the "free market system," even though the economic realities are of a very different kind. Or it could be that David is indeed a practitioner of these covenantal values. This reading of the verse would attest to the remarkable way in which David manages to value venturesome modes of governance together with sensitivity toward his subjects.

The third element here (vv. 16–18) shows that David is on his way to a bureaucracy (see also 5:13–15). What we might especially observe is the presence of Cherethites and Pelethites, that is, hired mercenaries. That note supports the claim of v. 13 that David "won a name for himself." The mercenaries embody the autonomy that the formula seems to suggest. That is, the wars of David do not need popular support, only the revenue to pay people to do the king's bidding. Obviously we are a considerable distance from the truth of the tribe when Israelites gladly joined the chieftain (Judges 5:2, 9). Now we call this a paid, voluntary army, when there is enough alienation between government policy and the perception of the citizenry that another way must be found to implement state policy. Worth noting is that the formula of v. 13 is specifically reminiscent of Gen. 11:4 and the Tower of Babel story, another instance in which it is possible to make one's own name. It is as though this narrative cannot quite make up its mind whether to present a faithfully Yahwistic picture or one that is more crassly in keeping with the way kings operate. Perhaps that vacillation is what makes the story both interesting and important.

NARRATIVE ART

Our study concerns narrative and the work of story theology. In the strictest sense, what we have been considering in this chapter is not fully appropriate to our subject. These texts contain little that shows narrative art as we commonly understand it, but that fact itself is important for understanding state truth.

The capability of story, the capacity to tell and hear story, is related to political, economic, and social factors. That is, our main learning about David in this rendering may be that something disastrous happens to good story when it is shaped to serve ideological claims of an imperial order. That surely is the message of Heym. Something happens when *imagination* is placed in the service of *ideology*, when it must always be pressed to a conclusion of a particular kind, when indeed the outcome is known before the story begins. As Gunn has seen so well,[30] the power of the David story is that it is not compelled to move to a certain conclusion. But, of course, Gunn comments on the Succession Narrative, not on these pieces. If artists have censors watching over them, one may get acceptable art, but it will scarcely reflect the freedom that belongs to good art.

That, I suspect, is an important consideration for us, not only as we try to understand these texts of state truth, but as we try to pay attention to who we are and what our capabilities and limitations are for the embrace of faith. That the key factors are political and economic is important. I think we must be very cautious of any romantic anthropology that finds differences of textual articulation in general cultural evolution or in the development of mental or moral processes. No doubt there are transformations of consciousness, but that is always closely connected to the technical development and the social forms of organization and power. Narrative is not an internal act in which we work out of our private imagination. It is an external public communication that is possible only in the parameters of public life. What we have seen here are the ways in which public communication is changed in Israel with the coming of kingship.[31] By setting these texts alongside the Succession Narrative, it is clear that public communities can take many forms and not everything needs to be submerged to state truth. But surely the undertaking of narrative in such a context is not only problematic but subversive.

STATE TRUTH TODAY

Finally, four concluding observations about our own practice of state truth are in order. First, it is these texts of state truth, especially 2 Samuel 7, that have provided for much church faith the taproot of a high Christology. Much church theology is another form of state truth, even if we call it "church truth." That is, much faith expressed in Jesus, who is the new David, tends to be a flat assertion that covers over the ambiguities and incongruities of the story. It is interesting to reflect on how different the faith of the church would have been had we derived the main claims from the narratives of tribal truth or the truth of the man, rather than the truth of the state.

Second, the David-Jesus linkage is not the only learning we may have for our own time for this narrative, because state truth is not all religious in our time. We must be concerned not only with excessive religious certitude, but with the state truth which is capitalist propaganda that fashions our public mind, that generates censorship of subtle kinds, and that flattens our imagination for purposes of consumerism.

Third, Karl Marx and Sigmund Freud in different ways have seen that the story "out there" becomes the story "in here." Peter Berger and Thomas Luckmann[32] write of the internalization of objectified truth, so that it comes to be "my story" as well as "our story." The point to make is that in our society we become walking, living enactments of state truth in quite personal ways. Religious certitude and public censorship generate individual persons who enact these stories in lives of inhumaneness and rigidity. The practice of narrative asks whether in such a society the truth of the tribe and the truth of the person can be told and are worth telling as forms of alternative truth.

Finally, in this assault on narrative that displays ideological tendencies, we may observe that the new censored articulation does not fully preclude the creative operation of language. That is, even these texts that seem to be deliberately flat and one-dimensional cannot keep it completely so. We cannot tell how much of the subtleness of the text is deliberate and how much of it is in spite of the authors. But there are interesting juxtapositions, ones which perhaps escaped the censor. Thus we have "David made a name" set against "Yahweh gave victory"—an odd combination, whether intentional or not. Or to say that David practiced justice and righteousness, and then to mention armed mercenaries, is a remarkable literary conclusion. Perhaps this is intentional communication. More likely, the dull, insensitive voices of the regime said things they themselves did not intend and did not know they were saying. But either way, we are not thereby given permission not to notice. Even in such less promising texts, the story does from time to time have its own powerful say, even against the agents of control. We can observe that even the truth of the state is not as sure as it first seemed. In the midst of state truth, there are irrepressible hints of other truth. State truth is like receiving cash from a bank teller. You count it and then hand it back and say, "You gave me $20 too much." The teller blinks and without looking pushes it back toward you and says, "This bank does not make mistakes."[33] One does not know what to do with such sure, unambiguous, state truth. One does not know if it is a gift, an error, or a bribe.

4

THE HOPEFUL TRUTH
OF THE ASSEMBLY

(PSALMS 89, 132; LAMENTATIONS 3:21–27; ISAIAH 55:3; 1 CHRONICLES 10—29)

Now I WANT to turn to more derivative presentations of David, those that engage in more overtly *theological constructions*. By that I do not mean to imply that the texts already considered are not theological constructions. Indeed, that has been the primary point of the discussion, that each is a construction serving a special theological agenda. But in what follows, the constructive element is more obvious and more generally acknowledged. I refer here specifically to: (1) the royal, liturgic promises that derive from David and from 2 Samuel 7 in particular, and (2) the ecclesial tradition of Chronicles. In considering these traditions, I move away from several things. First, in terms of our narrative agenda, we move away from the brilliant narratives that occupied us in the stories of "the Rise" and "the Succession." In making that move, clearly we no longer have stories that are so playful, imaginative, and impressionistic as the ones already considered. Second, in terms of historical issues, we move into texts for which historical reliability is not so highly rated. Indeed, these texts seem to create a different David, one which seems not so close to facticity. Our interest is not finally literary, for then we would not want to move to less powerful narrative. Nor is our interest ultimately historical, for then we would not want to move to less reliable texts. Rather, our interest is of another kind: the shape of truth as offered and proposed in each text. Given that agenda, we are not hindered by the measure of literary or historical value of the text.

What we have is *a* truth of David, *another* truth of David discerned, according to critical judgment, in approximately the fifth century. No one of these truths of David is a priori "more true." Each one needs to be received as best as it can, given its own articulation, art form and context, and its intentionality. We may believe that every such text was valued by some community as "truthful."

Under the rubric of the *hopeful truth of the assembly*, I will deal first with texts that derive from 1 Sam. 25:28 and 2 Sam. 7:24–16: Psalm 89, Isa. 55:3, Lam. 3:21–27, and Psalm 132. All of these articulate the promise to David affirmed by the tribe (1 Sam. 25:28) and by the state (2 Sam. 7:14–15), but now radically transformed. Second, I will then consider the text of 1 Chronicles 10—29 as one treatment of the David memory that is peculiarly aimed at a religious community.

THE HOPED-FOR DAVID

The truth of this literature now under consideration is a theological-ecclesial truth. The old political promises are remembered, but now are presented in a transformed mode to speak a new truth to the community in a changed circumstance. To be sure, the "truth of the assembly" is not devoid of political realism and ambition. But the political dimension is now cast in a different way. This "truth" no longer thinks in terms of state or kingdom or empire, for we are dealing with texts that mostly are set in a context of exile, or after exile, when such political notions have lost their power. Now the texts think primarily of a community of faith gathered around a future derived from David, but this David is no concrete help for politics and no concrete threat to the Babylonian or Persian overlords. Imperial dreaming is now precluded. The horizons of imagination must be of a different kind, necessarily shaped for a self-conscious *religious* enterprise.

By "truth of the *assembly*" I refer to a *religious* community, as distinct from a political community. "Assembly" refers to religious community, originally Jewish—but then also Christian—which has no ground to hope for political preeminence but can realistically be a community of faithful practice and anticipation. That at least is a mode of existence left free by the controlling empire. It is a modest historical existence, but viable.

I have called this *hopeful truth*. The phrase suggests two things. First, "hopeful" opens a way for eschatology, pointing to the Messiah who is to come, or for Christians, to the Messiah who is to come again. This truth is not about a remembered David, but it is about an *anticipated* David who will restore well-being to the historical process. The David spoken of here is not the one with historical scars nor the one with raw power. This David is the ideal David—as the real David should have been—and will now finally be. This David is, of course, a human agent, but one completely available for God's dreams which he bears, uncontaminated by any self-serving or ambiguity. The very name of David in these traditions asserts that God has dreams and intentions, that history is not closed, and that the person of David is a means for God's purpose to come to fruition in the future.

It is evident that this "hoped-for David" is a bold theological project. Perhaps that is why these texts do not trouble excessively with historical precision. We are not dealing here with a specific David, as the tribal and painful truths presented him, nor with the securely embodied David of state truth. Rather, this David is the imagined David who is a project of God's will for the future.

The second meaning of the word "hopeful" refers to a kind of uncritical acceptance of the text, an attitude that "hopes all things, believes all things, endures all things" (1 Cor. 13:7). This is a narrative that had believed much and endured much from David and still hoped for the very best to come out of David. One can see this operate in the Books of Chronicles, where the Samuel version has largely been purged and Israel now remembers what is most promising and most promissory about David.

One other comment about the hopeful truth of the assembly: These texts, as distinct from story as such, tend to be *liturgic* constructions growing out of and intended for liturgical processes. That is, some of the factors that operate in our normal "history-like"[1] scholarship have been and must be suspended. All of the characteristics of "hopeful truth" I have named thus relate especially to liturgical action. Hopeful truth is: aimed at religious community, open to the future, uncritical about a paradigmatic best.

The David given here, and the world of David presumed here is *liturgically shaped*. That is, these are images, pictures, and scenarios that Israel experienced in public worship. The public worship lying behind these texts is not a sober description of what is, but a visionary, evocative portrayal of what will be. The David of these texts is not obvious to everyone in this dismal historical setting, but is the David trusted and hoped-for by this community which could find little to value in its actual circumstance.

This means that liturgy makes it possible for Israel in such circumstances to practice the poetic presentation of an alternative world, alternative to the given world of exile and postexile. This liturgical activity is a stubborn refusal to accept the notion that the world is an unalterable given. It insists that the world can be alternatively reconstructed. Indeed the very act of liturgic portrayal is the offer of an alternative. The world in which the faithful live is not directly experienced, but is mediated through the bold creativity of liturgy, which asserts "it could be this way." The world of David, as any other world mediated to us, is socially constructed. These texts, as much as any we consider about David, are in fact actions of and residues of a social construction of reality, making available an alternative world of Davidic reality in which Israel may live. I submit that such a Davidic reality intends to counter not only the oppression of an alien state and the hopelessness of exilic powerlessness but also the loss of identity among the Diaspora.[2] Against all of these temptations to diminish life, the hopeful truth of David guards dignity, consolidates community, and bestows hope on a situation that might lead to despair.

STEADFAST LOVE AND A
SURE HOUSE

I explore this eschatological, ecclesiological handling of David in two quite different directions. The first of these focuses on the key phrase of the Davidic promise in 2 Sam. 7:15–16 (au. trans.):

> My *steadfast love* I will not remove
> as I removed it from Saul.
> Your house and your kingdom will be sure forever.

This text becomes the generative source of a great deal of theological reflection.[3] There is no doubt that 2 Sam. 7:14–16 is the pivotal text. It gathers up all the claims of the tribe and makes available the hope of the assembly. We linger over this text as the source of what is claimed in the assembly.

This text of 2 Sam. 7:14–16 is not given *ex nihilo*, however. Nathan's oracle about a "*sure* house" sounded already in the tribal narrative. In 1 Sam. 25:28, the vision of the tribe is placed in the mouth of Abigail:

> The Lord will certainly make my lord *a sure house*, because my lord is fighting the battles of the Lord; and evil shall not be found in you so long as you live.

This statement is embedded in Israel's early narrative. We may suggest that here we are at the primal claim of the tradition. The claim made by Abigail is also heard in 1 Sam. 26:23; 27:12.[4] These three texts evidence the emergence of Davidic theology in an early form. Already here, the words "sure" (*'emeth*) and "steadfast love" (*ḥesed*) are operative. They stand at the beginning and starting point of a theological trajectory which then becomes more disciplined, more sophisticated, and probably more cynical.

On the basis of these rather straightforward tribal assertions, the state has tailored in a formal style the claim of 2 Sam. 7:14–16. For reasons of state, the primal tribal hunch about David has now become a formal, stylized, programmatic statement on which is based the legitimacy of the regime. The state formulation of this truth, as we have noted, escalates the claim from the tribe. Now it is not only a "sure house." Now it is guaranteed that the Lord's "steadfast love" (*ḥesed*) will never be withdrawn. That claim is beyond any notion the tribe had, moving, as the regime always must, in the direction of permanence.

Nonetheless, as we have also seen, state truth is indeed a vehicle for and a bearer of real truth, albeit presented for tendentious and skewed reasons. Thus, after the state, the assembly was able to find in these claims an enduring truth that had power and pertinence to its new situation. In these texts then we consider how that enduring claim had its say, now freed from its more propagandistic function. We consider derivative texts that look back to 1 Sam. 25:28 and 2 Sam. 7:14–16, but which move in different directions.

Psalm 89

Our first text is Psalm 89, a liturgical reflection and commentary on the oracle of 2 Samuel 7. Some hold it to precede 2 Samuel 7, but here I take it to be later and derivative. Psalm 89 is an important and quite complex liturgic piece, and we cannot here consider it in detail. The most we can do is to notice the use of the double formula of *sure* and *steadfast love* (*'emeth* and *hesed*) of 2 Sam. 7:15–16.

In both 1 Sam. 25:28 and 2 Sam. 7:14–16, the words *hesed* and *'emeth* have been decisive. Psalm 89 makes extensive use of the terms. First they are used to characterize Yahweh's way in general. Then they are used to articulate the peculiar role occupied by David who is the special object of Yahweh's faithfulness. Thus, the two words characterize the peculiar force of David as a bearer of Yahweh's fidelity. This word pair apparently had programmatic importance for those generations that experienced the collapse of the Davidic monarchy as a bearer of Yahweh's fidelity.

The uses in Psalm 89 are as follows (au. trans., using English versification):

I will sing of thy *hesed* [plural] . . .
   I will proclaim thy faithfulness [*'amûnah*]. . . .
                                   (v. 1)

Thy *hesed* was established for ever,
   thy *'amûnah* is established in the heavens.
                                   (v. 2)

Let the heavens praise thy wonders [*pela'*]
   thy *'amûnah* in the assembly of the holy ones.
                                   (v. 5)

Who is as mighty as you, Yahweh,
   with thy *'amûnah* round about?
                                   (v. 8)

Righteousness and justice are the foundation of your throne,
   hesed and *'amûnah* go before thee.
                                   (v. 14)

My *'amûnah* and my *hesed* shall be before him,
   and in my name he shall be exalted.
                                   (v. 24)

I will not remove from him my *hesed*,
   nor be false in my *'amûnah*.
                                   (v. 33)

Yahweh, where are your *hesed* [plural] of old,
   which by this *'amûnah* you did swear to David?
                                   (v. 49)

It is clear that this psalm is a reflection or meditation of a liturgical act based on the basic assertions of 2 Samuel 7. In almost all of the uses of *hesed* and *'amûnah* the two words are parallel. In v. 8, there is only *'amûnah* without *hesed*, the parallel is *hasîn* ("strength"). In v. 14, the word pair is used in parallel to another set, *mišpaṭ* and *ṣedeqah*, but the main usage is with this pair.

The word pair is used in very different ways in various parts of Psalm 89. First, it is used as a doxology to Yahweh, without any reference to the dynasty or any other historical experience (vv. 1, 2, 5, 8, 14). These uses make the most cosmic claim and envision this reality in a heavenly scope, as v. 5 mentions the divine council, "the holy ones." In v. 8, this is still the case, though the rhetoric draws things closer to Israel's experience with the phrase "Yahweh of hosts," and in v. 14 the words are used in a royal metaphor, referring to God's throne. But in all such cases, the interest is singularly on Yahweh, which contrasts with the usage of 2 Samuel 7, where attention is turned from Yahweh to dynasty.

Only at the very end of the first unit (v. 18) is there mention of "our king," so that we receive the first intimation that all of this is to be aimed at the royal, dynastic reality in Israel. Thus the argument proceeds along very different lines, establishing that *hesed* and *'amûnah* are dimensions of Yahweh's inclination, and not simply commitments to David. Thus the first use is properly theological, not yet derivatively political.

The psalm makes an abrupt move in a dynastic direction in v. 19. Then (*'az*), that is, in David's time, you spoke to your faithful ones (plural), presumably David. The shift from mythological to historical process is made in the clear linkage to David. This dynastic reference is confirmed in v. 24 where the precise formula of 2 Samuel 7 is repeated. What an enormous rhetorical move in which the features exalted about the character and person of God are now reassigned to David and to David's house! In v. 24 *hesed* and *'emeth* are lodged with him and in v. 33 they are not to be removed. In v. 37 the dynasty is said to be as "firm" (*ne' emān*) as a witness in the sky.

The third kind of usage of this word pair is a surprise. The psalm ends in a lament (vv. 46–51), for the throne is now in sore straits. The speaker appeals to the promise which no longer seems to be valid. The question is put:

> Lord, where is your *hesed* [plural] of old,
> which by your *faithfulness* you swore to David?

The lament is quite concrete, referring to David by name, and Yahweh is here being held to his own promise. The insistence is not unlike the prayer of David in 2 Sam. 7:18–29 which also holds Yahweh to his own commitment. Only here, there is more pathos, reflective of a more desperate situation. In contrast, the prayer of David in 2 Samuel 7 is still buoyant and prior to any pathos.

Thus we may trace the expression, *hesed* and *'amûnah*, from the *tribal enthusiasm* of Abigail (1 Sam. 25:28) to the *symmetrical assurance* of the oracle (2 Sam. 7:16) to the *liturgical insistence* of this psalm. Psalm 89 makes the claim ontologically, that is, rooted in the very reality of God. On the one hand, it celebrates this commitment, and on the other hand, it recognizes its problematic character. The psalm is clear that the guarantee is unconditional and without reserve, and the loss of this unconditionality hints at a question of theodicy. The truth borne by David is Yahweh's profound and unqualified commitment to this family and therefore to this people. Psalm 89 ends in lament, because the premise seems not to "work." Historical reality cannot measure up to such an unqualified hope.

It is not possible to place this psalm historically. Aubrey Johnson[5] most unambiguously treats the crisis as a cultic crisis. Artur Weiser thinks it may be historical, but before 587.[6] Hans Joachim Kraus places it in a cultic setting, but does see it as a historical crisis, before 587.[7] For our purposes it is enough to see two things. On the one hand, the main claims of state truth are powerfully present and functioning. On the other hand, these main claims are now in deep jeopardy. No resolute conclusion is drawn here, but Psalm 89 does put us on notice. Even the power of state claim does not keep the raw reality of life from surfacing. It is rather the certitude of state truth that evokes the question of theodicy, for the realities rarely coincide with the formulas.

Lamentations 3:21–27 and Isaiah 55:3

The anticipation of Abigail (1 Sam. 25:28) resurfaces in 2 Samuel 7 and Psalm 89, especially to serve the exilic community which was profoundly unsure of Yahweh's support and reliability after 587. In this move we may identify two uses that make this deep hope available to exiles (Lam. 3:21–27; Isa. 55:3).

Lam. 3:21–27 is a psalm remarkably crafted as an acrostic poem, having three consecutive lines for each letter of the alphabet. Verse 18 announced that "my hope [*tohaltî*] is gone." Then there is an amazing break in v. 21.

> But this I call to mind,
>> therefore I hope ['*ôhî*'];
> The *hesed* [plural] of Yahweh never cease,
>> his mercies never end;
> they are new every morning;
>> great is thy faithfulness ['*amûnah*].
> Yahweh is my portion.
>> Therefore I hope ['*ôhîl*] in him.
>> (Lam. 3 21–24, au. trans.)

The one for whom hope is utterly gone (v. 18) becomes the one who hopes, only two verses later (v. 21). The turn occurs because the speaker remembers that the *hesed* never cease. It is hard to determine, but I suspect that v. 22 should be in quotes. That is, the speaker is not recalling a general idea or a pleasant generality, but is quoting a text, and the text quoted is surely the oracle of 2 Samuel 7 or some derivative form of it. The citation of that text becomes the ground for a complete turnabout in the entire poem. It is in the moment of David, unqualified or untroubled by the "if " of Psalm 132, that Israel found a deep hope in time of exile. But the reference is not simply a historical one—the remembering of Nathan's oracle. It is also a literary one— the quotation of a text which this community does not doubt, even though the text collides with all the surrounding historical data. This usage then, along with Psalms 89 and 132, is a good example of a text using a text as a theological resource.

To be sure, there is no mention here of king, throne, or dynasty, but that is why this is a hopeful truth. It would be a less compelling hope if one had to be so concrete and specific as to speak of restored David, because then historical factors would need to be given greater play. But the allusion to David is sufficient to let desperate exiles believe that Yahweh's *hesed* (plural) abide and are not nullified even by such a disaster. The "steadfast love" (*hesed*) promise to David has a fuller, freer form in these derivative texts.

Out of that decisive memory now used for a very different purpose comes the rest of the poem which has overcome self-doubt and which has a vigorous confidence in Yahweh, evidenced by the series of "Thou" statements in vv. 57–66. The poem is clear that Yahweh holds the initiative for the future against every circumstance.

The second demonstration of this move is Isa. 55:3, a promise at the very end of exilic Isaiah, which speaks about transformed creation. In this verse the entire hope is rooted in the same reference to 2 Sam. 7:14–15:

> Incline your ear, and come to me,
>   hear, that your soul may live;
> and I will make with you an everlasting covenant [berîth 'ôlam],
>   my steadfast, sure love for David [ḥasdê david hanne' 'emānîm].

Again the word is plural, ḥasde, along with the accompanying adjective. There can be no doubt that the exilic poem looks back to 2 Samuel 7, for the reference to David is explicit. But the point made in this text is very different. In an influential article, Otto Eissfeldt[8] has argued that Psalm 89 is to be taken literally and concretely. It envisions a future well-being which is dynastic. But in contrast, says Eissfeldt, Isaiah 55 breaks with that specific form of hope, and uses the promises of 2 Samuel 7 in a metaphorical way to characterize the whole people of Israel who now share in the promise. It is now upon the whole community, without confinement to the Davidic house, that the Davidic promises are pronounced.

Psalm 132

It is widely recognized that Psalm 132 lives in considerable tension with Psalm 89.[9] The entire psalm seems to be concerned with the settlement of the ark in Jerusalem, thus linking it closely to the narrative of 2 Samuel 6. The agenda of the ark suggests that the primary concern is not the *dynasty* but the *presence*. Yet Israel links together temple presence and dynasty, so that it is difficult to think about the temple without the king who seems to come with it. In Ps. 132:11, the promise of 2 Samuel 7 and Psalm 89 is reiterated in the rather familiar form:

> The Lord swore to David a sure oath ['emeth]
>   from which he would not turn back:
> "One of the sons of your body
>   I will set on your throne."

The language is slightly changed, but the substance is unmistakable.
The promise is the same. If the psalm had stopped with this promise,
we could handle this text right along with Psalm 89. But this version
in Psalm 132 continues in a strange manner in v. 12:

> If ['im] your sons keep my covenant
> and my testimonies which I shall teach them,
> their sons also for ever
> shall sit upon your throne.

In this one rhetorical move of v. 12, everything is changed. It is the
adding of an "if " of the Torah, reminiscent of the Mosaic covenant.
(See the very same move with reference to the dynasty in 1 Kings 2:4).
In that simple move all the grand claims of state theology are profoundly
compromised, if not completely abandoned and nullified. The Davidic
claim is subordinated to the Mosaic claim. Sociologically the importance of this move can hardly be overstated. State truth is judged by
old tribal truth which is always more severe and demanding. It will
be remembered that Saul was finally jeopardized because he did not
obey. He did not conform to the "if." Now in this text, the Davidic
occupant on the throne is subjected to the same demanding conditional
which places everything in jeopardy.

The point is not to argue that Psalm 132 is superior to Psalm 89
(though my Protestant inclinations are in that direction). It is rather
to see that David's truth, even when formulated by the state, is filled
with ambiguity, and that there continued to be conflict over it. One
cannot just pick one of these texts in preference to the others. Rather,
we need to recognize that each has its claim and its social function,
and none may be taken as the "true exposition" of 2 Samuel 7, simply
because we prefer it so.

What is clear is that different voices and different interests in Israel
must have experienced and therefore articulated the promise in different ways. The party of reform and severity[10] must have reintroduced
the Mosaic condition. But Psalm 89 reflects a very different pastoral
sensitivity, a concern to find a sure grounding for the community when
all other ground is sinking sand.[11]

Thus, we may suggest that 2 Samuel 7 becomes a hope articulated
in three very different ways, all of which seek to hold the truth of
David:

Psalm 89 is an explicit, concrete dynastic hope which continues to believe that the dynasty will be restored. I submit that it is this tradition that speaks the truth of David in quite explicit messianic terms. But even this version of the truth is not untroubled, for the issue of theodicy begins to be heard. When the language of lament is used as in v. 46, with its anguished "how long," then we are at the brink of recognizing that God does not and has not kept all these promises and that the oracle of 2 Samuel 7 is not as clean and clear as Nathan and the ideologues would have us believe.

Isaiah 55:3 and Lam. 3:20–22 are a very different form of hope. They affirm that Yahweh continues to work for the sake of Israel. But it is not an anticipated future which has a precise historical shape, certainly not a royal shape. The hope is for a future to be received by the whole community but the shape of it is not known in advance. This tradition is much more theocentric. It believes that the commitment to David made by Yahweh is reliable and overriding, but it does not insist on a historical Davidic embodiment. It does not claim or need to know too much.

Psalm 132 is most distinct from the other two modes. It is an expression of the more rigorous party. Both by its reference to "covenant," a word not present in 2 Samuel 7, and by its use of "if," the future is understood to have moral dimensions, not articulated in the other two expressions.

In presenting a theological articulation of Davidic hope, one may not choose one of these to the neglect of the others, nor should one be reductionist about them, to force them all to agree. They should rather be left in their varied splendor. One may take this variety either as rich diversity that keeps the tradition pertinent in different circumstances, or as evidence that the community continued to be troubled. Both awarenesses of rich diversity and of troubled uncertainty are needed for doing biblical theology. The lack of these two tends to turn the Bible into a closed, ideological statement.

David is the bearer of the promise, the one who keeps the future open against every vexed present. The truth of David is a truth about a sure promised future. These four texts are an odd assortment and I do not wish to force them into a pattern unduly. These four texts all share the use of the dynastic formula, but they also seem to share a determined look to the *future*. Psalm 89 is still most closely linked to dynastic concerns, but the lament at the end evidences a crisis for the dynasty. Psalm 132 is close to Mosaic covenantal expectations, but it still asks about the future. More fundamentally, Isa. 55:3 and Lam. 3:20–22 utilize the David traditions precisely to offer hope to bereft exiles. The texts assert that the main truth about David is that God presides over this man, this dream, this promise into the future. Clearly none of the other literature we have studied had such a look to the future, surely because none of them faced such a stressful, failed present.

THE CHRONICLER'S DAVID

The hopeful truth of the assembly may be traced, as mentioned, in a second, quite distinct direction. The most consistently *ecclesiological* presentation of Davidic hope in the Old Testament is that of the Chronicler. We may begin with some critical considerations with regard to this literature, which inform our reading of it.

First, the Chronicler is, in the present form of the text, linked literarily to Ezra and Nehemiah. Since in much critical thought Ezra-Nehemiah is easier to place than is the Chronicler, these two works have been decisive for our placement and characterization of the entire literature. As a result, the entire corpus is understood in terms of the rebuilding of Nehemiah and the reforms of Ezra which, if not legalistic, are at least intensely devoted to the realities of the Torah. This Torah-shaped future, if it should be linked to David at all, would appeal especially to the Davidic version given in Psalm 132.

But some distinctions can be made in this literature. In 1961 David Noel Freedman[12] proposed (and was followed by Frank M. Cross)[13] that we may identify different layers of the Chronicler. Freedman proposes that the dominant shaping of the Chronicler was done around 515 in connection with the obscure activity of Zerubbabel and the work of Haggai and Zechariah, to support and enhance the restoration of Davidic Israel in the context of a rebuilt temple. This means that the main critical interest of the Chronicler, as urged by Freedman and Cross, is to separate this *royal* movement from the more Torah-oriented activity of Ezra and Nehemiah.[14]

Second, 1 Chronicles 1—9 constitutes a special interest and a special problem. These chapters are a genealogical summary of all that has gone before. They are of interest to us for the remarkable way in which all of history prior to David is so quickly summarized. The Chronicler has no interest in history until David appears and therefore it can be treated in such summary fashion. The structure of the text indicates that all of history has been waiting for David, who begins a new history—indeed the only history that matters to this religious community.

Everything else before David is preliminary and can be handled in a footnote. It is as though the whole universe has been waiting for this man and this moment. Now that may seem strange to us, but it is not different than the Marcionite tendency to begin history with John the Baptist without all of Israel before. It is not different than the tendencies of Reformation perspectives to imagine that history began with Luther and to be silent on the ancient and Medieval church. It is not different than the major American political parties who begin their historical recitals either with Jefferson or Lincoln. It is not different than any of us in psychotherapy who discover how selective and summarizing our functioning account of the past is. The whole universe, whose center is in Jerusalem, had indeed been waiting for this man and this moment.

Third, the historical placement and the mode of beginning the narrative suggest the intent of this "truth," organized around David.

1. We have yet another literature that organizes the entire history of Israel around the Davidic reality. Everything else is subsumed under this theme, as evidenced in the sheer quantity of material devoted to it, while other matters are harshly summarized or neglected altogether. David is the only real actor in the historical process.

2. The Davidic hope presented here is concrete and explicitly political and not at all metaphorical. That is, the function of David is to permit, authorize, and legitimate a religious community whose practice is theologically faithful and historically significant.

3. The hope expressed here is something of a practice of liberation theology. The counter-side of Davidic restoration is the rejection of Persian rule, benign as it may have been. Thus in a rather understated way, this is indeed subversive literature, nurturing a hope that runs counter to the present arrangement of social, political panic.

4. We must see this hope, as political as it is, as couched in a carefully redacted version that takes into account the new ecclesiological situation. Hope has been turned in a sectarian direction, precisely appropriate to the historical context of the literature. More directly, dynastic ambitions were subordinated to the realities of the Persian Empire.

There is no doubt that we are dealing with a hopeful truth (eschatological), but it is less clear whether it is a hopeful truth for a state or for an assembly. The narrative has some "itch" for the grandeur of the state's David. Yet there is historical realism, for this David does not do what a state David does. Instead, he leads a community of worship. The splendor of the narrative is that it asserts the profound importance of this new Davidic authorization. This Davidic form of truth has an amazing capacity to stay alive and pertinent in many different settings. It is able to be expressed in a variety of modes depending on the requirements and possibilities of the circumstance.

1 Chronicles 10—29

The Davidic materials in the Chronicler are found in 1 Chronicles 10—29. We may note first of all how the Chronicler has framed the materials at the beginning (chap. 10) and at the conclusion (chap. 29), and has treated the intervening materials and themes.

Beginning and End

1 Chronicles 10 marks the transition to the truth of David and provides entry into the narratives. One notices immediately that the First Book of Samuel is mostly ignored by the Chronicler. This truth of the assembly does not want to go back to the rawness of the tribe. It is content to live from the state, and it is glad for the lid that state truth has put upon the tribal versions which might contain embarrassments. The beginning point is only to give a favorable version of the transition. The first narrative disposes of Saul by telling of the suicide. The narrative is crafted so that David is not mentioned, and therefore could not be blamed, until v. 14. When David does appear, the narrative introduces him tersely: "Therefore the Lord slew him, and turned the kingdom over to David the son of Jesse" (10:14). David is completely unimplicated. It is as though he is an innocent bystander, who passively but willingly received the unsought gift of the kingdom. He did not

yearn or covet or seek or calculate. It was a free gift! And as we shall see, the David of the Chronicles understood himself that way and so accepted the gift of governance.

The whole of 1 Samuel is thus briefly summarized and dismissed. 1 Chronicles 10 serves only as a passing comment on Saul, because the Saul-David confrontation was of no interest in the context of the Chronicle. The remainder of 1 Samuel is only interspersed later where useful in anecdotal fashion. There is no sustained account and certainly no hint of David's intrigue or the tension that led to the crown. David's beginning is carefully expressed as Yahweh's action:

. . . turned the kingdom over to David the son of Jesse. (1 Chron. 10:14)

They anointed David king over Israel, according to the word of the Lord. (1 Chron. 11:3)

And David became greater and greater, for the Lord of hosts was with him. (1 Chron. 11:9)

This David tradition works to secure David well beyond the accidents of the historical process.

The final Davidic chapter (29) brings together David's faith and David's attention to cultic matters, for in the Chronicler, faith and worship belong intensely together. Indeed 1 Chronicles 29 itself reads almost like a liturgical sequence:

Verse 1 states the premise of the whole: surely the palace is not for humankind ('ādam) but for the Lord God.

Verses 2–5 are an invitation of *offer willingly* made on the basis of what David in his royal generosity has already done: I have provided (v. 2); I have provided, I have given a treasure, I have given (v. 3).

And then in v. 5, comes the appeal: "Who will offer self willingly?" (*mithnaddev*, au. trans.). This word expressed in the *hithpa'el* is worth noting. The root *nadav*, of course, is a standard word for a free-will offering, that is, one not calculated or coerced by the system. But the reflexive use is much stronger. It is used in our passage six times (vv. 5, 6, 9, [2], 14, 17), the primary cluster in the entire Bible. Thus this text makes the most massive statement about self-abandoned giving. The same word is used in the same tradition in 2 Chron. 17:16, where it refers to a military volunteer. Elsewhere it is used in Ezra 1:6; 2:68; 3:5; and Neh. 11:2, all of which pertain to the same general phenomenon of utter commitment to the renewed temple. The only use that falls outside this world is that in the Song of Deborah (Judges 5:1, 9) which refers to the "willing troop" of the Israelite peasants who follow the leadership of Deborah and Barak. Norman K. Gottwald,[15] following Chaim Rabin, proposes that the term is more than "volunteer," but refers to a "social-structure obligation of the levy . . . the success of the levy depends on the willing and speedy compliance of the several tribes when summoned." This is contrasted with a drafted army of state power. We should not, of course, make easy moves from the *old tribal practice* to the truth of the assembly of Chronicles, but the linkages might be important. What is called for here is not routine financial assessments for the cultus, but a sense of community solidarity around an urgent task about which there is a consensus.

Verses 6–8 then report a response of the people in generous giving, so that these verses are a structural response to the invitation of vv. 2–5.

Verse 9 offers a conclusion that the people gave willingly, and David rejoices. This verse corresponds to the initial premise of v. 1 so that the chapter has a chiastic structure. Verses 1 and 9 provide the envelope of the large claims and vv. 2–5, 6–8 are a practical and specific enactment of those claims.

This is followed in 1 Chron. 29:10–22 by a prayer and blessing: Verses 10–13 are a *doxology* to Yahweh in which everything is credited to Yahweh. Verses 14–17 are a corresponding act of *deference* in which David cedes everything to Yahweh and claims nothing for himself. This is articulated in v. 14, a quite-familiar formula: "For all things come from thee, and of thy own have we given thee." It is hard to imagine a more concise statement of genuine *doxology* and *deference* in which it is acknowledged that even the offerings offered willingly are only a return to the real giver. The comment continues to identify Israel now and in all times past as sojourners without an abiding place. (This act of deference is echoed in 1 Cor. 4:7 where Paul asks polemically: "What have you that you did not receive?") Note that I have used the terms *doxology* and *deference* here as I did in David's prayer in 2 Samuel 7. But here there is no demand. We are obviously in a very different climate. One has the impression that we are dealing here with a much more genuine act of faith than in the Samuel narrative. Verses 18–19 are a petition governed by three terms, "keep, direct, grant," asking that God make it possible for Solomon and Israel to be obedient. Even obedience is understood here as in the gift of Yahweh. Verses 20–21 are a festal act of sacrifice and blessing.

Notice that the concluding report on David concerns the liturgical activity of David. It takes no great imagination to see that this picture of David is drastically different from the portrayals given in the Samuel traditions. It is not hard to see that such a constructed picture of David surely serves the context of the fifth century and no doubt serves the specific claims of the Levitic priesthood. The truth about David given here is that David is a pious, cultic man who finds his life shaped and enhanced by such explicit religious commitment. He is indeed a "man of the assembly."

David's Truth Re-presented

Now we are in a position to consider the ways in which the Chronicler has selected and arranged material to present this dimension of David's truth. The material is, as we have seen, framed so that David's public life begins in *unexpected gift* (1 Chronicles 10) and culminates in *extravagant commitment* (1 Chronicles 29). The remainder of the material operates between the initial gift and the culminating commitment.

David's truth is offered in a purged and censored fashion. These are materials *taken over from the Samuel narratives*. Some are taken over as they stand, without tampering or modification. Among these is the anecdote of 2 Sam. 23:12,[16] now placed in 1 Chron. 11:15–19. In both contexts the narrative shows David in noble solidarity with his commanders. This is in contrast to his violent treatment of Uriah, reported in the "painful truth" but noticeably absent here. What interests us here is that the same episode has been strategically placed at the very beginning of the David narrative. It now functions as a decisive characterization with much more intentionality than was evident in the original usage of 2 Samuel.

We may note three other passages in which the Samuel materials are used, but with important changes. 1 Chronicles 17 repeats most of 2 Samuel 7. Perhaps the main point to observe is that in 17:13, there is no longer any mention of punishment or chastisement for sin. In 1 Chron. 20:1 the Bathsheba-Uriah incident is completely deleted. It is clear that this tradition is aware of the incident. The narrative begins with repetition from 2 Samuel 11:

> In the spring of the year, the time when kings go forth to battle, Joab led out the army, and ravaged the country of the Ammonites, and came and besieged Rabbah. . . . And Joab smote Rabbah, and overthrew it. . . . Then David and all the people returned to Jerusalem. (1 Chron. 20:1, 3)

1 Chronicles 21 repeats 2 Samuel 24 on the census and the necessary punishment. It is remarkable that this is portrayed in most of its rawness. But, as is well known, the introduction of Satan (1 Chron. 21:1) again shields both God and David from anything negative. These three passages are the only narrative material drawn from 1 Samuel.

What is clear is that the Chronicler has removed the linchpin of the whole history of David as previously presented. One cannot believe this act was unwitting. The point is that this is a very different David, a literary construct, surely as much as the other one, but with a very different theological intentionality. This David is a completely obedient man without self-assertion or moral ambiguity. This is the David that is necessary for the authorization of a faithful religious community. The point to observe here is a simple one: this hopeful truth about David lives in profound tension with the old tradition. It borrows from the old tradition, learns from it, and fights against it, as it brings to speech a radically new truth about David.

Cultic Reality

The second and most dominant material is not the traditional narrative taken from the earlier account. What interests the Chronicler and occupies most of the space is interest in the cultic apparatus, the temple and *the proper worship of God*. There are openings for this in 1 Chronicles 13 and 15 on the movement of the ark, which appeal to old stories. In 15:16–24 there is a long and characteristic list of officials. In chap. 16 there is a recital of the officials (vv. 4–6) and then Psalm 105 appears, followed by more cultic data in vv. 37–42. We may not take this placement of Psalm 105 simply as a redactor's decision, though it is possible. It is also the truth about David.[17] It announces that David's sense of reality is essentially a liturgical commitment. We need not regard that announcement as inferior or to be lightly dismissed.

1 Chronicles 22—25 contain extensive materials related to worship. Chapter 22 shows support being mobilized for the temple. Then comes a stretch of new material. Chapter 23 is an authorization for the *Levites*. One can observe that even here the tradition struggles with the priority of the Aaronides and must acknowledge them. But the Levites are vigorously set alongside them. Chapter 24 concerns the Aaronides, but v. 20 makes room for the Levites. Indeed v. 6 is grandly ecumenical, presenting a vision of all the priestly order in community together. Chapter 25 concerns the musicians and all those who made the worship proper and legitimate.

The narrative has the amazing capacity to link the most sweeping theological claims to what appears to be quite routine matters of *cultic reality*. Thus in the midst of all this tedious provision, David says to Solomon in 1 Chron. 28:20:

> Be strong and of good courage, and do it. Fear not, be not dismayed; for the Lord God, even my God, is with you. He will not fail you or forsake you, until all the work for the service of the house of the Lord is finished.

The language of David's charge is not strange to us. This is the most standard form of Levitic preaching (as Gerhard von Rad[18] and Jacob M. Myers[19] have noted). We recognize it as old war language, coming out of holy war traditions. Only Solomon is not directed here to win a great battle or act heroically against an enemy. Rather the charge is that he build the temple. This language is thus used for a general theological assurance. This David has now entrusted to Solomon his most important mandate. But it is noteworthy that this charge is immediately followed in 1 Chron. 28:21 by a cultic provision:

> And behold the divisions of the priests and the Levites for all the service of the house of God; and with you in all the work will be every willing man who has skill for any kind of service.

This tradition of liturgical foundation may have great visions, but it also has a heavy dose of realism. It knows that ordered, *well-administered human resources* go along with the *promise of God*.

Dominant Themes

This rather hasty survey is sufficient for us to note and articulate three dominant themes for the David of this material in Chronicles.

First, David is a man of genuine piety. No doubt this required some imaginative conjuring on the part of the assembly. It required passing over in studied silence some of the motifs of the older memory. Yet we dare to say that the credibility of this claim for David is based in a secure reality. It is not made up of whole cloth. There was a strand of powerful piety in the memory of David, as for example in his repentance in 2 Samuel 12. This pious David here becomes an important exemplar for this postexilic community struggling to find a way to be a faithful assembly. What better way than to have David become the model for the faith and piety that is now required?

In the second place, David is in constant attentiveness and fidelity to Yahweh. Concerning the person of David, this surely looks back to the old tribal claim that Yahweh will be with him. Indeed, the entire memory of David is clear on this point. Surely there is more to him than royal ideology. It is a fact of the life of this extraordinary man. At the same time, this attentiveness is peculiarly important to this community now gathered around the memory of David. Every other support had now failed these Jews. It was important to present God— the God of David—as reliably committed to David and to David's people.

In the third place, the piety of David and the fidelity of Yahweh are given shape and mediated through the cultus. With the failure of state propaganda, the capacity of public liturgy to give to Jews a visible world becomes important. David is, therefore, presented as a man committed to the assembly and Yahweh is surely the God mediated through liturgic practice. This emphasis is generally absent in the other David materials we have studied, but now the world has been fully entrusted to the liturgy. The truth of David this community can trust is liturgic truth. This is now the vehicle for David and the social reality authorized by him. David and David's community are known here crucially by being "at worship."

Summary

I have traced two derivative traditions concerning David, *the eschatological messianic David* of the *hasdê* ("acts of fidelity") of the monarchy (Psalms 89 and 132; Lam. 3:21–27; Isa. 55:3) and *the ecclesiastical*

David of the Chronicler. There is no easy or obvious way that these two trajectories can by themselves be held together. They go in very different directions. Yet I suggest that both of them portray a David filled with hope who permits a community of faith to be sustained in an alien, if not hostile, environment. It is the case that David becomes an important point of reference in the period of "small things" (Zech. 4:10) after the exile, as he emerges during the exile as a point of appeal. Both the *"acts of fidelity" tradition* and the *Chronicler tradition* intend to claim that in the person, character, and role of David, something decisive has happened that qualifies the events of history. This is more obvious in the "acts of fidelity" tradition, for in Lam. 3:18–22 and Isa. 55:3–5, this faith in David's promise is used to refute present circumstances.

The matter is not as clear in Chronicles. It may be (as Paul D. Hanson[20] suggests) that eschatology here is realized rather than anticipatory. Or it may be (as James D. Newsome[21] argues) that the links of Haggai and Zechariah make this tradition dangerously and immediately anticipatory in its outlook. Either way, the Chronicler's version of David believes that both present and future are inevitably to be David-shaped.[22] The last paragraph of Chronicles (2 Chron. 36:22–23) is important in this regard. It provides a link to the opening verses of Ezra, but even if we ignore that connection, which is perhaps a late arrangement, the point of an open future is suggestive. According to 36:21, the exile is to fulfill the judgment word of Jeremiah. According to 36:22 (again according to Jeremiah) there will be a homecoming. And the homecoming is precisely to Jerusalem. If Chronicles is designed to urge a valuing of Jerusalem, then the links to Zerubbabel and the entire Haggai-Zechariah vision is credible. The David tradition is used in a most unexpected way to refute both the intransigence of Babylon and the possible indifference of Persia, along with the despair of Judah. This tradition finds remarkable energy for the future in the Davidic materials. Indeed for these voices, it is impossible to see a future for the community apart from the future seeded in the Davidic tradition.

What makes the truth of the assembly hopeful is that it does not engage in political calculation or strategy. The possibilities through the political process are not valued. Rather, in such a marginal situation without political leverage, these traditions depend directly on God's faithfulness to create a public life of faith It is a hope that is turned only to God and against every other form of hope. It is religious affirmation that both present and future belong precisely to God. The agent who makes God's governance of both present and future historically possible is David. It is David who is Israel's primal history maker, even in the assembly so long removed from David's own time. The powerful memory of David is now shaped so that it mediates a fresh future to Israel.

CONCLUSION:
TRUTH FREE, IN JEOPARDY

DAVID IS INDEED the dominant engine for Israel's imagination. The literature and the faith of Israel are endlessly fascinated with David. The David of the tradition continues to generate new historical possibilities, always beyond those presently given. We have in these various texts found David's truth, but we have found that truth to be as elusive as powerful, as ironic as it is affirmative.

We have traversed a sweep of material, with a rich variety of theological aspects:

The Trustful Truth of the Tribe: 1 Sam. 16:1—2 Sam. 5:5 (chap. 1)
The Painful Truth of the Man: 2 Samuel 9—20 and 1 Kings 1—2 (chap. 2)
The Sure Truth of the State: 2 Sam. 5:6—8:18 (chap. 3)
The Hopeful Truth of the Assembly: Psalms 89; 132; Lam. 3:21–27; Isa. 55:3; 1 Chronicles 10—29 (chap. 4)

First, we have observed *how richly varied* the tradition is. Different generations were able to locate in the memory of David different resources that let them live faithful lives. Each one of these articulations of David is genuinely authoritative.

In line with this, the tradition may not *be collapsed or reduced* to a single claim, or made to agree. Nor should we make judgments about which is superior or inferior or original or derivative. We are, as noted, inclined to do that on historical grounds, with our passion for "the original," or on literary grounds, with our artistic canon of excellence.

But if our criterion be the truth of David—that is, what has been found of power and fidelity in this memory—*then we must be more reticent and careful about either historical or literary reductions.* For who can say who has best discerned who the real David is? In our modern propensity for psychology, I expect we would mostly be drawn to the Succession Narrative, the only piece that hunches about the interiority of David. But that is not necessarily a statement about the relative merit of a text. It is more likely a statement about us and our times. No doubt in a different circumstance and context, like the Chronicler, we would find that the liturgical David carried a "truer truth." The point of course is that *each* David must be honored, valued, and taken seriously on his own terms, each as a distinct rendering of this fascinating character.

Finally, I cannot resist an attempt to make a generalized statement. Our study presses us to ask, what is it that makes David endlessly fascinating to us? Why is it that the tradition has not lingered over Saul or Solomon or anyone else the way it has lingered over David?

I propose to think this way. On the one hand, David is much like us. There is something genuinely human about him, which means that there is a shape to his life that we can count on and identify with. There is also a freedom about him that make. him interesting and not boring. But even while we are able to identify with him, there is distance between David and us. That distance is because of his nerve and grandeur in which he can make the great gesture that carries everyone before him. And yet in the midst of the *grand gesture*, there is a *tough faith* that permits this one to yield in simple ways that seem genuine and not contrived. There is, then, the ability to identify with and yet to be called out beyond ourselves, for we know we are in the presence of greatness.

How could we catch the imaginative power of this man remembered? After having warned about reductionism, I want to engage in it. I suggest we do not turn to the Succession Narrative as might be our wont, but that we take 1 Chron. 29:14 as a summary of this man:

> For all things come from thee,
> and of thy own have we given thee.

That statement may be a liturgical construction that has nothing to do with David historically, but I suggest it may catch something of the enduring quality of David, that all of life is a gift that may be impinged upon and exploited but also honored.[1] Though there are incredible variances in the tradition, there may be a focus to all of it. Contrasted with Moses (who is the other great figure of the tradition), David is the one who can *receive and relinquish with some graciousness*. David is not a fanatic. He does not scruple excessively, and so he is the one who has a chance in public life. We see this expressed in all four groups of text we have examined.

1. The tribal claim of David, that is, "The Rise of David," presents a receiving David in 1 Sam. 16:1–13. In v. 11 he is dependent, deferential (*qaton*). That quality is persistent in his dealings with Saul, even if it is calculating.

2. That same motif of receiving and relinquishing is faced by David in torturous ways in the Succession Narrative. It is evident in the repentance of 2 Sam. 12:13 in which David clearly understood that life is not to be lived on his own terms. It is also reflected in the remarkable statements of 2 Sam. 15:25–26 and 16:12, in which David puts his life in God's hands.

3. In the state claims, the gift is clearly unilateral and unmerited (7:8–16) and is received that way in the "deferential" prayer of 7:18–22, in which the term *qaton* is used, albeit differently. David receives and claims much more than he is prepared to relinquish.

4. It is not different in the religious claim of Chronicles, in which the promise is again unilateral (1 Chronicles 17) where the term *qaton* is used (vv. 16–17) again to put things in perspective.

Thus I suggest that the act of *emptiness and trustful surrender* in 1 Chron. 29:14 articulates a leitmotif that all of these traditionists have found in David. To be sure, it is liturgically cast. It is highly stylized. But what gives fascination to this character, ruthless and cunning as he is, is that there is a trusting naiveté that yields enormous power. In my theological tradition, we would call that "grace."

But of course David is not a theologian, so I would not use the word "theology" in any technical sense, but instead point to a statement of graciousness in the little narrative of 2 Sam. 23:14–17. In an act of simple majesty and nobility, David refuses to drink water secured at the risk of his men's lives, even though they went into risk in utter devotion to him. David's response is not one of rejection, but of solidarity. His act of pouring water out on the ground could have been read as refusal of the gift. But David's men knew better. They knew it was a sacramental act because words would fail to speak about the binding between them. It is worth noting that the anecdote is retained in 1 Chron. 11:17–19. As we have seen, Chronicles is inclined to purge such anecdotal material. But this story is not only retained by the Chronicler but it is also placed at the beginning, in the very first chapter on David. The Chronicler knew that this anecdote, of all that might be lost or retained, could not be omitted because it discloses the truth of this man, as only story can do.

My suggestion is that the David traditions contain many alternative modes, but perhaps they are caught between the brackets of 2 Sam. 23:14–17, *David's amazing human sensitivity and solidarity*, and 1 Chron. 29:14. *David's profound yielding to God*. No wonder he is in favor with God and humankind. The two decisive qualities of *amazing human sensitivity* and *profound yielding to God* are not unrelated. Together they are the truth that this tradition most prizes and most wants to announce (cf. 1 John 4:20–21). This concerns us, for they are the truth most urgently yearned for in our time.

It will be evident that I have not ventured toward the New Testament. Obviously there is much more there that could claim attention in relation to our theme. It lies beyond the task we have set for ourselves.

I cannot, however, resist one linkage. We have been concerned with the question of David's truth. The phrase, as we have said, is intended to be ambiguous. It might invite historical investigation into the historical reality of David, scars and all, that is, the truth about David. Partly we have asked about that—but not centrally. Or it might mean the truth by which David lived, his personal faith upon which he relied. But we regard that as beyond our reach so this is no quest in that sense. Then, too, it might mean David's truth as the disclosure of reality which clusters around the person of David, the moment of truth made possible because we linger over this memory and this hope. In some ways our investigation has tilted toward all three, but our concern has been the third, the disclosure of reality which clusters around the person of David. It is truth embodied in the man, and mediated through his life.

In the tale of Jesus, Pilate—governor, manager of imperial intelligence with a monopoly on knowledge—has finally asked, in the presence of Jesus, "What is truth?" (John 18:38). Likely the Fourth Evangelist intends all three of these questions:

What is the factual matter about Jesus?

What is the truth to which Jesus clings?

What is the disclosure of reality which clusters around this person Jesus?

Pilate's question of course admits of no simple answer except that Jesus had already offered himself as the singular form of truth (John 14:6).[2] That question of Pilate stands at the end of the tale. At the beginning, it has already been announced that this one is full of "grace and truth" (1:14). If we refer to the Hebrew behind the Greek formula, *charis kai alētheia*, we have a formula which sounds very Davidic, *hesed we'emeth*.[3] The terms are a cliché in Israel, but the pair is present in 2 Sam. 7:14–16 concerning David.

It is grace and truth (*hesed we'emeth; charitos kai alētheia*) that causes David to pour out water in solidarity (2 Samuel 23:14–17; 1 Chron. 11:15–19). It is grace and truth that leads David to recognize that all gifts are given back to the real giver of all (1 Chron. 29:14). It is grace and truth, that enigmatic combination of reliability and playfulness, that requires continuing probing, that permits ongoing articulation, and that legitimates narrative as the only way to express what is sure and yet open. And when we finish, we are still much like Pilate. We know this meeting with "grace and truth" is the real thing, but we wonder about its reliability. David keeps evoking the question, so that life will not be settled either in the despairing fear of Saul or the shameless confidence of Solomon.[4] Truth of a Davidic kind is always at the dangerous edge of deception or ideology, always remarkably free, yet always open to risk and in jeopardy. A flatter truth than that could not attest to this restless man. A surer truth than that would deny this man his eagerness for what is yet promised.

NOTES

INTRODUCTION

1. See David Tracy, *The Analogical Imagination* (New York: Crossroad, 1981), 99–229. He has characterized a religious "classic" as a piece of literature to which the community of faith assigns authority and to which it returns again and again for life and faith. In that sense, David is a "classic" in the biblical community, though Tracy speaks only of literature and not persons.

2. That the tradition is a construction is an exceedingly important point that touches upon crucial hermeneutical issues. It is not necessary to be so hypercritical as Edmund Leach: "Anthropological Approaches to the Study of the Bible During the Twentieth Century," in *Harmonizing America's Iconic Book*, ed. Gene M. Tucker and Douglas A. Knight (Chico, Calif.: Scholars Press, 1982), 74–77. Such scholars are excessively committed to Enlightenment modes of historicality which are not relevant for our consideration. That the David presented here is not a description but a portrait matters enormously. On the matter of portrait, see Walter Brueggemann, "The Book of Jeremiah: Portrait of the Prophet," *Interpretation* 37 (1983): 130–45. And note the word "portrait" in the title of Elie Wiesel's *Five Biblical Portraits* (Notre Dame, Ind.: Univ. of Notre Dame Press, 1981).

3. On the power of imaginative personal construction, see Roy Schafer, *Language and Insight* (New Haven, Conn.: Yale Univ. Press, 1978).

4. On theological dimensions of such dramatic rendering, see Dale Patrick, *The Rendering of God in the Old Testament* (Philadelphia: Fortress Press, 1981).

5. On the dramatic, theological power of this text, see Paul Lehmann, *The Transfiguration of Politics* (New York: Harper & Row, 1975), 48–70.

6. On the communal, creative aspect of disclosure, see H. Richard Nie-

buhr, *The Meaning of Revelation* (New York: Macmillan Co., 1941). Likely Niebuhr understated the generative community in the disclosing process, for the community is much more than the receiver of the disclosure. It is also articulator. It is in the act of articulation that the disclosure is evoked, that was not until then evoked.

7. John L. McKenzie, *The Old Testament Without Illusion* (Chicago: Thomas More Press, 1979), 236.

8. Samuel Terrien, *The Elusive Presence: Toward a New Biblical Theology* (New York: Harper & Row, 1979), 282.

9. Tracy, *Analogical Imagination,* chap. 6, has provided an exhaustive bibliography on the subject.

10. We are only at the beginning of our study of what imagination means for exposition. But it does seem clear that very much interpretation which seeks only a single, persistent meaning is pornographic in denying freedom to the text. On imagination and pornography, see Matthew L. Lamb, "The Challenge of Critical Theory," in *Sociology and Human Destiny*, ed. Gregory Baum (New York: Seabury Press, 1980), 185–98.

11. On the paradigmatic role of David for Israel, see Walter Brueggemann, "David and His Theologian," *Catholic Biblical Quarterly* 30 (1968): 156–81.

CHAPTER 1

1. It is agreed by many scholars that 1 Sam. 16:1–13 is not a part of the original narrative, but has been placed there only later. See P. Kyle McCarter, Jr., "The Apology of David," *Journal of Biblical Literature* 99 (1980): 502 n. 25.

2. The exact point of the ending in chap. 5 is unclear. See ibid., 489–93. See David M. Gunn, *The Story of King David,* Journal for the Study of the Old Testament, Supplement 6 (Sheffield: JSOT Press, 1978), chap. 4. He makes a quite different division of the material, but his judgment is a significant departure from conventional scholarly opinion.

3. Artur Weiser, "Die Legitimation des Konigs Davids," *Vetus Testamentum* 16 (1966): 325–54.

4. McCarter, "Apology of David," 489–504. See his more detailed discussion in his important commentary, *I Samuel*, Anchor Bible 8 (Garden City, N.Y.: Doubleday & Co., 1980).

5. Niels Peter Lemche, "David's Rise," *Journal for the Study of the Old Testament* 10 (1978): 2–25. He offers a complete bibliography. Particular note should be made of J. H. Gronbaek's study cited there.

6. Norman K. Gottwald, *The Tribes of Yahweh: A Sociology of the Religion of Liberated Israel 1250–1050 B.C.E.* (Maryknoll, N.Y.: Orbis Books, 1979), 323–37. He writes:

> In specifically Israelite terms, we must view its tribalism as a form chosen
> by people who consciously rejected Canaanite centralization of power and

deliberately aimed to define their own uncentralized system against the effort of Canaanite society to crush the budding movement. Israel's tribalism was an autonomous project which tried to roll back the zone of political centralization in Canaan, to claim territory and peoples for an egalitarian mode of agricultural and pastoral life. (Pp. 324–25)

To be sure, Gottwald writes concerning the situation of Joshua and not that of David, and the two are different. Nonetheless, the David enterprise includes some of the same dimensions as are evident in the Israelite discussions of kingship.

See James W. Flanagan, "Models for the Origin of Iron Age Monarchy: A Modern Case Study," Seminar Papers (Chico, Calif.: Scholars Press, 1982), 135–56. He has argued that David's power is a strange combination of king and tribal chieftain. In the narrative of the rise to power, he is much more chieftain than he is king.

7. On the power of civility for social control, see Joseph Cuddihy, The Ordeal of Civility (New York: Basic Books, 1974).

8. Lemche, "David's Rise," 23 n. 31.

9. George Mendenhall, The Tenth Generation: The Origins of the Biblical Tradition (Baltimore: Johns Hopkins Press, 1973), 135–36.

10. Ibid., 69–104.

11. Ibid., 83.

12. On the development of counter-truth and indeed, counter-canon, see my discussion in The Creative Word (Philadelphia Fortress Press, 1982), chap. 3. Note especially the references to Susan Weber Wittig and Carol P. Christ in Soundings 61 (1978). The David stories in this literature are articulations of a counter-truth that solidified community and legitimated an alternative perception of reality, alternative to Canaanite and Philistine perceptions and finally also alternative to that of Saul.

13. This community, like every community, wants to externalize and objectify its definition of reality. This has been clarified best by Peter Berger, The Sacred Canopy (Garden City, N.Y.: Doubleday & Co., 1969) and Peter Berger and Thomas Luckmann, The Social Construction of Reality (Garden City, N.Y.: Doubleday & Co., 1967).

14. I have already noted that this unit is commonly taken as later. I do not dispute that critical judgment. Its presence here, however, is all the more intentional for that reason and now has the function of introduction and initiation. See Martin Kessler, "Narrative Technique in I Sam. 16:1–13," Catholic Biblical Quarterly 32 (1970): 543–54.

15. On this text and this entire piece of literature, see the "close reading" of Peter D. Miscall, The Workings of Old Testament Narrative (Philadelphia: Fortress Press, 1983), 50–138. Robert Alter, The Art of Biblical Narrative (New York: Basic Books, 1981), 148–49, has observed that "see" is a Leitwort for this narrative. It is important that in this verse Yahweh announces, "I have

seen for myself a king." Alter translates the line, "I have chosen." He makes that translation in order to make a contrast between "choose" and "reject." I am not sure, however, that this is the most telling rendering. The conventional translation is "provide." The same usage is made in Genesis 22. See my comments on that usage in *Genesis* (Atlanta: John Knox Press, 1982), 191–92. There I have argued, following Karl Barth, that "provide" is a nice English rendering for "pro-video," "to see ahead," that is, providentially. In any case, the word is peculiarly important.

16. On narrative as a mode of peculiar importance for marginal ones, see John Dominic Crossan, "Paradox Gives Rise to Metaphor," *Biblical Research* 24–25 (1979–80): 20–37. Crossan makes most suggestive comments on the sociology of narrative.

17. See Lemche, "David's Rise," 4–5. There is evidence to suggest the giant was killed by Elhanan (2 Sam. 21:19), but this name may be confused with or identified with David. The facticity of the matter is not available underneath the complicated layers of narrative material.

18. See McCarter, "Apology of David," 492. Note that the Masoretic Text has a much more extended narrative than does the Septuagint. Whatever textual judgment be made, there is clearly extensive redactional activity.

19. The "beasts" are no doubt meant literally. But in the way of biblical metaphor, "beast" also means capricious political power. Cf. Ezek. 34:17–19, 28. Thus the move from "beast" to Goliath is well contained within the development of the metaphor, for he is an embodiment of "beast" in the political experience of Israel.

20. See Gottwald, *Tribes of Yahweh*, 414–17.

21. On the use of the formula, see Walter Zimmerli, *I Am Yahweh* (Atlanta: John Knox Press, 1982), 66.

22. Gottwald, *Tribes of Yahweh*, 585.

23. This episode may also not be "original," even as the other two passages we have considered. McCarter ("Apology of David," 493) convincingly regards it as a tendentious retelling of the narrative of chap. 26, so that David is even more positively presented. Such a critical judgment does not carry us very far, however, because we are responsible for the text as it now is given to us.

24. See David M. Gunn, *The Fate of King Saul*, Journal for the Study of the Old Testament, Supplement 14 (Sheffield: JSOT Press, 1980), 93–96.

25. Alter, *Art of Biblical Narrative*, 36–37.

CHAPTER 2

1. Leonard Rost, "Die Überlieferung von der Thronnachfolge Davids," in *Das Kleine Credo und andere Studien zum Alten Testament* ([Heidelberg: Quelle and Meyer, 1965], 119–253 [= Beiträge zur Wissenschaft vom Alten und Neuen Testament 3, 1926]). He first named the narrative.

2. Aage Carlson, *David the Chosen King* (Uppsala: Almqvist and Wiksells, 1964).

3. Brevard S. Childs, *Introduction to the Old Testament as Scripture* (Philadelphia: Fortress Press, 1979), 276.

4. Alter, *Art of Biblical Narrative*, 119 n. 1.

5. Alter writes, ". . . the personal voice of a shaken David begins to emerge" (ibid., 119).

6. This change on David's part is to be carefully distinguished from any "evolution of consciousness" which is now so fashionable. For as that is currently presented, it is understood as leading to new freedom and autonomy. Clearly David's "emergence" is in exactly the opposite direction, toward anguish, guilt, and terror, not buoyancy.

7. Gunn has summarized the alternatives suggested by scholars in *The Story of King David*, chap. 2.

8. The discussion is well summarized by Gunn (ibid., 21–26). Note especially the fact that L. Delekat and R. N. Whybray can draw antithetical conclusions from the same text. That attests either to scholarly confusion (which I do not believe) or to the skill of the narrators, which I take to be the point.

9. See Gerhard von Rad, "The Beginning of Historical Writing in Ancient Israel," in *The Problem of the Hexateuch and Other Essays* (reprint ed., London: SCM Press, 1984), 176–204. Von Rad has written the classic statement of the achievement of this literature as a breakthrough in narrative presentation and the attendant psychological understanding that comes with that literary breakthrough.

10. On an attempt to interpret an earlier form of the narrative in a way appreciative of Saul, see W. Lee Humphreys, "From Tragic Hero to Villain: A Study of the Figure of Saul and the Development of I Samuel," *Journal for the Study of the Old Testament* 22 (1982): 95–117.

11. See my attempt to present David as a model figure in a pivotal moment between the fearfulness of Saul and the profanation of Solomon (*In Man We Trust* [Atlanta: John Knox Press, 1972]).

12. See Brueggemann, "David and His Theologian." See the perceptive critical comments of Jack R. Lundbom, "Abraham and David in the Theology of the Yahwist," in *The Word of the Lord Shall Go Forth*, ed. Carol L. Meyers and M. O'Connor (Winona Lake, Ind.: Eisenbrauns, 1983), 203–9.

13 Following von Rad, B. David Napier has offered a most articulate and sensitive exposition of this sequence of episodes (*From Faith to Faith* [New York: Harper & Brothers, 1955], chap. 3).

14. On this text see George Ridout, "The Rape of Tamar," in *Rhetorical Criticism*, ed. Jared J. Jackson and Martin Kessler (Pittsburgh: Pickwick Press, 1974), 79–98, and most recently Burke O. Long, *Images of Man and God* (Sheffield: Almond Press, 1981), 26–34.

15. See Charles Conroy, *Absalom, Absalom!*, Analecta Biblica 81 (Rome: Biblical Institute Press, 1978), and David M. Gunn, "From Jerusalem to the Jordan and Back: Symmetry in 2 Samuel XV–XX," *Vetus Testamentum* 30 (1980): 109–13.

16. On the contrasting motifs of life and death in the Joseph and Succession narratives, see Walter Brueggemann, "Life and Death in Tenth Century Israel," *Journal of the American Academy of Religion* 40 (1972): 96–109.

17. On the crucial and delicate match between substance and mode of articulation, see Brueggemann, *Creative Word*, in which I have explored some major examples of this in the Old Testament literature.

18. The notion of enlightenment in the Solomonic period is a construct proposed by von Rad, which has been exceedingly influential. See Gerhard von Rad, *Old Testament Theology* (New York: Harper & Row, 1962), 1:48–56, to which he has made appeal in a number of other works. That construct has come under heavy criticism, especially from James Crenshaw in his influential article, "Method in Determining Wisdom Influence Upon 'Historical' Literature," *Journal of Biblical Literature* 88 (1969): 129–42, and *Studies in Ancient Israelite Wisdom* (New York: Ktav Publ., 1976), 16–20. Gunn has supported Crenshaw's critique (*Story of King David*, 26–29).

19. Von Rad, "Beginning of Historical Writing," 204.

20. Ibid.

21. See Karl Barth, *Protestant Theology in the Nineteenth Century* (Valley Forge, Pa.: Judson Press, 1973) chaps. 2–4. Barth has analyzed this issue most convincingly.

22. Gunn has put it well (*Story of King David*, chap. 3). He insists that the narrative is "entertainment." By this term Gunn means to deny any ideological or partisan motivation. But he also insists that it is entertainment that is "serious," that it "challenges their intellect, their emotions, their understanding of people, of society and of themselves" (p. 61). In that sense it is "subversive" of conventional presuppositions. And though Gunn does not use such terminology, I think he would agree with that characterization.

23. On the function of narrative as shattering as well as constructing, see Paul Ricoeur, "Toward a Hermeneutic of the Idea of Revelation" (in *Essays on Biblical Interpretation*, ed. Lewis S. Mudge [Philadelphia: Fortress Press, 1980], 73–118), and a programmatic statement of "redescribing" in "Biblical Hermeneutics," *Semeia* 4 (1975): 29–148.

24. Von Rad, "Beginning of Historical Writing," 198.

25. On a critique of the destructive consequences of such a notion, see Daniel Yankelovich, *New Rules, Searching for Self-Fulfillment in a World Turned Upside Down* (New York: Random House, 1981), chap. 23 and throughout.

26. Martin Noth (*The Deuteronomistic History*, Journal for the Study of the Old Testament, Supplement 15 [Sheffield: JSOT Press, 1981], 56–57), assigns it to the Deuteronomist.

27. See Carlson, *David the Chosen King*, 126, who makes some astute theological observations that move beyond Noth's assignment to sources.

28. The pursuit of the interiority of David is not unlike that of Raskolnikov in Feodor Dostoevski's *Crime and Punishment*, in which the real agony is not

that offered by institutional authority but by what is offered within the man. It is that "interior judgment" that finally destroys.

29. See Walter Brueggemann, "On Coping with Curse: A Study of 2 Sam. 16:5–14," *Catholic Biblical Quarterly* 36 (1974): 175–92.

30. David's refusal to take direct, personal vengeance perhaps relates to the intent of the narrative to enhance the state. In order to govern, the state must maintain a monopoly of vengeance. It would not do then to have any character, least of all the king, in a royal narrative, exercising private, personal vengeance.

31. Alter, *Art of Biblical Narrative*, 76, writes, "It is brilliant transitional device. It firmly ties in the story of David as adulterer and murderer with the large national-historical perspective of the preceding chronicle."

32. A parallel to this device may be found in 1 Kings 21. The narrative really reaches its obvious conclusion in v. 16, for the issue of the plot has been resolved. But in v. 17, after that conclusion, the word of the Lord appears by Elijah. Theologically only now is the issue put. Rhetorically, the appearance of the prophet enables the story to continue, else it would have ended. It is the same in the David story.

33. On the world-shattering function of parable, see John Dominic Crossan, *The Dark Interval* (Niles, Ill.: Argus Communications, 1975). Crossan has since published more extended and more technical studies, but this is something of a classic for current discussion.

34. The requirement of parable in the face of power is analogous to speaking the gospel to a thoroughly enculturated church. See Fred Craddock, *Overhearing the Gospel* (Nashville: Abingdon Press, 1978). He has explored the theme of "overhearing" the gospel, after the manner of Søren Kierkegaard. Direct communication is sure to be co-opted, so another form must be found.

35. Patrick D. Miller, Jr., *Sin and Judgment in the Prophets*, Society of Biblical Literature Monograph Series 27 (Chico, Calif.: Scholars Press, 1982), 83.

CHAPTER 3

1. A. F. Campbell, *The Ark Narrative*, Society of Biblical Literature Dissertation Series 16 (Missoula, Mont.: Scholars Press, 1975).

2. Gunn, *Story of King David*, chap. 4.

3. Carlson, *David the Chosen King*.

4. Alter, *Art of Biblical Narrative*, 119 n. 1.

5. Gottwald, *Tribes of Yahweh*, 293–337.

6. Gottwald (ibid., 584–87 and throughout) has argued that Israel occupied a peasant situation produced from the inequality of economics sanctioned and legitimated by the state that had a monopoly both on goods and on the means of production. "Peasant" refers to an economic mode of life in which "surplus

value" is regularly used by others at the expense of the producer. As this paper was reaching final form, I have seen the superb discussion of James W. Flanagan, "Social Transformation and Ritual in 2 Samuel 6," in *The Word of God Shall Go Forth*, ed. Meyers and O'Connor, 361–72. Flanagan provides, in my judgment, a sturdy critical foundation for the point of my argument. First, he sees that the material represents a sharply changed social situation:

Israel was released from subservience by the events described in 2 Sam. 5:13—8:18. Under David's leadership, the Yahwists moved from defense to offense, trading status as beleaguered prey for that of empire building. . . . The transition toward centralized supra- and extra-tribal administration signaled class and social distinctions which would inevitably bestow economic and political advantage upon a core of elite specialists. . . . Social scientists have in fact singled out legitimacy as the primary indispensable stabilizer for new authority structures and have noted that the need to legitimate is especially pressing when the new structures do not rest easily upon traditional values. (Pp. 363–64)

Second, Flanagan has suggested (to my knowledge the first such suggestion) a coherent literary structure indicating that this is an intentional literary piece and not a random collection. Such an intentional structure would correlate with a substantive intentionality. He proposes six elements which fall into three pairs (p. 361):

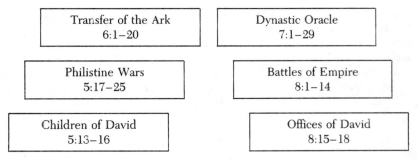

Transfer of the Ark 6:1–20	Dynastic Oracle 7:1–29
Philistine Wars 5:17–25	Battles of Empire 8:1–14
Children of David 5:13–16	Offices of David 8:15–18

Each pair shows a displacement and an ascending dominance. Flanagan rightly and discerningly concludes (following Terrence Turner): There is "an iconic relation between the structure of rituals and that of the social transitions they mediate . . ." (p. 369). I should add not only ritual structure but also literary structure mediates social transition to new forms of social power.

7.   Frank M. Cross, *Canaanite Myth and Hebrew Epic* (Cambridge: Harvard Univ. Press, 1973), 237–41. See also George Mendenhall, "The Monarchy," *Interpretation* 29 (1975): 155–70.

8.   Stefan Heym, *The King David Report* (New York: G. P. Putnam's Sons, 1973). On the works of Heym, see the comments of Walter S. Hollenweger, "The Other Exegeses," *Horizons in Biblical Theology* 3 (1981): 155–60.

9. Heym, *King David Report*, 39. Siegfried Herrmann, *Time and History* (Nashville: Abingdon Press. 1981), 61, rejects Heym's critical judgment. But I do not believe Herrmann's critical objection touches Heym's hermeneutical judgment.

10. M. I. Steblin-Kamenskij, *The Saga Mind* (Odinse: Odense Universitets Verlag, 1973).

11. Ibid., 21.

12. The shift from oral to writing society is a crucial factor in Walter Ong's understanding of the history of culture. That cruciality of cultural change is reflected in the more popular work of Marshall McLuhan, a student of Ong. On a vigorous dissent from the view of Ong, see Herbert N. Schneidau, "The Word Against the Word: Derrida on Textuality," *Semeia* 23 (1982): 11–12.

13. The capacity for critical distance from perceived reality, which is at the heart of the distinction between syncretic and state truth, is reflected in a variety of studies. As this pertains to Scripture study, see especially the important discussion of Gary A. Herion, "The Role of Historical Narrative in Biblical Thought: The Tendencies Underlying Old Testament Historiography," *Journal for the Study of the Old Testament* 21 (1981): 25–57.

14. A notorious case of state truth to maintain ideology is reflected in William Greider, "The Education of David Stockman," *Atlantic Monthly* 248 (December 1981): 17–54, in which it is clear that a cynical presentation of "facts" believed not to be true are necessary for the maintenance of monopolistic claims.

15. On the systematic function of propaganda. see Jacques Ellul, *Propaganda: The Formation of Mens' Attitudes* (New York: Alfred A. Knopf, 1965).

16. For a discerning exposition of this text, see Eugene March, "II Samuel 7:1–17," *Interpretation* 35 (1981): 397–401.

17. On the nature of that conflict and its settlement, see Baruch Halpern, "The Uneasy Compromise: Israel between League and Monarchy," in *Traditions in Transformation*, ed. Baruch Halpern and Jon D. Levenson (Winona Lake, Ind.: Eisenbrauns, 1981), 59–96.

18. See the caustic remarks of Sam J. Ervin, Jr., *The Whole Truth: The Watergate Conspiracy by Sam Ervin* (New York: Random House, 1981), chap. 3, on the matter of "Executive Privilege." The chapter is entitled "Executive Poppycock."

19. John M. Lundquist has offered a vigorous analysis of the uses the temple has for the regime ("What Is a Temple? A Preliminary Typology," in *The Quest for the Kingdom of God*, ed. H. B. Huffmon, F. A. Spina, A. R. W. Green [Winona Lake, Ind.: Eisenbrauns, 1983], 205–18).

20. See Otto Eissfeldt, "The Promises of Grace to David in Isaiah 55:1–5," in *Israel's Prophetic Heritage*, ed. Bernhard W. Anderson and Walter Harrelson (New York: Harper & Row, 1962), 196–207. He has shown how the Davidic promise was first applied to the family and dynasty, and only later was democratized.

21. On the "if" of covenant faith, see the form-critical analysis of James Muilenburg, "The Form and Structure of the Covenantal Formulations," *Vetus Testamentum* 9 (1959): 347–65, in which the "if" is shown to be structurally decisive. That conditional quality of covenantal faith has been well explicated by David Noel Freedman, "Divine Commitment and Human Obligation," *Interpretation* 18 (1964): 419–31.

22. See Robert Polzin, *Moses and the Deuteronomist* (New York: Seabury Press, 1980), 36–43. He has shrewdly observed how the incomparability of Yahweh is claimed with its intended derivative, the incomparability of Israel, or even more its leader, Moses. Polzin's analysis pertains to the claims of Moses, but in our text the claim made for the incomparability of David and the dynasty seems to be made in the same way.

23. On the propensity of the state to absolutize its claims as "forever," see the critical analysis of Henri Mottu, "Jeremiah vs. Hananiah: Ideology and Truth in Old Testament Prophecy," in *The Bible and Liberation: Political and Social Hermeneutics*, ed. Norman K. Gottwald (Maryknoll, N.Y.: Orbis Books, 1983), 235–51.

24. On the problem of drawing too near to God and the reassertion of God's freedom and distance, see Werner E. Lemke, "The Near and the Distant God," *Journal of Biblical Literature* 100 (1981): 541–55.

25. Herbert Marcuse has well articulated how the control of language is crucial to the political control of the regime. See *One Dimensional Man* (Boston: Beacon Press, 1964), chap. 4.

26. On the structural function of the adverb, see Muilenburg, "Form and Structure of Covenantal Formulations."

27. Heym, *King David Report*, 141–43.

28. On the value of holiness and purity by those who maintain the status quo, see the comments of Fernando Belo, *A Materialist Reading of the Gospel of Mary* (Maryknoll, N.Y.: Orbis Books, 1981), chap. 1, esp. 53–59.

29. Heym, *King David Report*, 143.

30. See Gunn's comments with particular reference he makes to the analysis of Shakespeare by L. C. Knights (*Story of King David*, 25–27).

31. It is worth reflecting on the ways in which technology changes communication, in light of current interest in narrative. Narrative is a mode of communication which works mightily against reducing communication to technique. And this is written just as *Time* magazine (January 1983) has named "The Computer" as "Man of the Year"!

32. Berger and Luckmann, *Social Construction of Reality*, chap. 3.

33. Alexander Solzhenitsyn, "An Incident at Krechetovka Station" (in *Stories and Prose Poems* [New York: Farrar, Straus & Giroux, 1971], 167–240), has a shrewd discerning story about state truth. At its conclusion, the Security Officer announces the ultimate claim of state truth: "Your Tverikin's being sorted out all right. We don't make mistakes" (p. 240). I am grateful to Gail O'Day for this reference.

CHAPTER 4

1. On the category of "history-like," see James Barr, *The Scope and Authority of the Bible*, Explorations in Theology 7 (London: SCM Press, 1980), 1–17. Barr acknowledges that he is making use of the analysis of Hans W. Frei, *The Eclipse of Biblical Narrative* (New Haven, Conn.: Yale Univ. Press, 1974), who has written the definitive work on the problem.

2. See Sara Japhet, "People and Land in the Restoration Period," in *Das Land Israel in Biblischer Zeit*, ed. George Strecker, Göttinger Theologische Arbeiten 25 Göttingen: Vandenhoeck & Ruprecht, 1983), 103–25. She has provided a helpful analysis of the cultural situation which required such theology.

3. See the analysis of this group of texts by Jean M. Vincent, *Studien zur Literarsischen Eigenart und zur geistiger Hermat von Jesaja, Kap.* 40–55, Beiträge zur Biblischen Exegese and Theologie (Bern: Peter Lang Verlag, 1977) and the convenient summary statement on p. 83.

4. See the provocative study of Matitiahu Tsevat, *The Meaning of the Book of Job and Other Biblical Studies* (New York: Ktav Publ., 1980), 101–17. I agree with much of his analysis of 2 Samuel 7, though I find it difficult to follow him in finding there a pre-dynastic understanding of Davidic covenant.

5. Aubrey Johnson, *Sacral Kingship in Ancient Israel* (Cardiff: Univ. of Wales Press, 1967), 106–11.

6. Artur Weiser, *Psalms* (Philadelphia: Westminster Press, 1962), 591.

7. Hans Joachim Kraus, *Psalmen 2*, Bibel und Kirche 15, 2d ed. (Neukirchen: Neukirchener Verlag, 1961).

8. Eissfeldt, "Promises of Grace to David in Isaiah 55:1–5."

9. See, e.g., Tsevat, *Meaning of the Book of Job*, 108–9.

10. Paul D. Hanson, *The Diversity of Scripture* (Philadelphia: Fortress Press, 1982), 16 and throughout, uses the word "reform" to refer to radical prophetic-apocalyptic tradition.

11. Hanson refers to this "sure grounding" as the reality of "form" which he finds in the continuities of the faith.

12. David Noel Freedman, "The Chronicler's Purpose," *Catholic Biblical Quarterly* 23 (1961): 436–42.

13. Frank M. Cross, "A Reconstruction of the Judean Restoration," *Journal of Biblical Literature* 94 (1975): 12–18.

14. See H. G. M. Williamson, "Eschatology in Chronicles," *Tyndale Bulletin* 28 (1977): 120–33. He has subjected this approach to a severe criticism and has found it wanting.

15. Gottwald, *Tribes of Yahweh*, 539 n. 457.

16. See Williamson, "Eschatology in Chronicles," 134–42, for a careful comparison and contrast of the two chapters.

17. See the shrewd suggestion of Gary A. Herion, "The Role of Historical Narrative in Biblical Thought," *Journal for the Study of the Old Testament*

21 (1981): 40–42, on the function of this psalm as a way of appropriating the tradition in a sociologically suggestive way.

18. Gerhard von Rad, "The Levitical Sermons in I and II Chronicles," in *Problem of Hexateuch and Other Essays*, 243–66.

19. Jacob M. Myers, "The Kerygma of the Chronicler," *Interpretation* 20 (1966): 159–73.

20. Paul D. Hanson, *The Dawn of Apocalyptic* (Philadelphia: Fortress Press, 1975), 276.

21. James D. Newsome, "Toward a New Understanding of the Chronicler and His Purposes," *Journal of Biblical Literature* 94 (1975): 201–17.

22. Williamson, "Eschatology in Chronicles," 153–54.

CONCLUSION

1. David M. Gunn, "David and the Gift of the Kingdom (2 Sam. 2–4, 9–20, 1 Kgs. 1–2)," *Semeia* 3 (1975): 14–45, already in an early article had seen that the tension of "gift-grasp" is the crucial one for the Davidic tradition. Gunn, of course, does not carry that into the New Testament. But if one were to do so, one would find a very close parallel in structure in the hymn of Phil. 2:5–11.

2. See the discussion of this text by Paul Lehmann, *The Transfiguration of Politics* (New York: Harper & Row, 1975), 48–78.

3. On the pair, *ḥesed* and *'emeth*, see Edgar Kellenberger, *Ḥasad wa' 'emat als Ausdruck einer Glaubenserfahrung* (Zurich: Theologischer Verlag, 1982).

4. See my statement concerning David at this delicate point in *In Man We Trust*, chap. 4.